Uncle Tim's
Book of Chords

A Complete Visual Guide To Basic Chords For The Guitar

By Tim Gillespie

Published by

Mountain Studios
1025 Oakdale Place
Boulder CO 80304

© Copyright 2002 Mountain Studios
All Rights Reserved

D1441755

Uncle Tim's

Book of Chords

A Complete Visual Guide To Basic Chords For The Guitar

By Tim Gillespie

Published by:

Visualize Great Music

Mountain Studios
1025 Oakdale Place
Boulder CO 80304-0749

All rights reserved. No part of this book may be reproduced or transmitted in any form
or by any means, electronic or mechanical, including photocopying, recording
or by any other information storage and retrieval system without the written permission
from the author, except for the inclusion of a brief quotation in a review.

First Printing 1998
Second Printing 1999
Third Printing 2000
Fourth Printing 2001
Fifth Printing 2002

Printed in the United States

© Copyright 2002

Photography © by Mountain Studios 2002
All Rights Reserved.
All photography by Terry Asker

Library of Congress Card Catalog Number 97-092762
ISBN 0-9647059-5-8 $19.95

Thanks Sara!

Table Of Contents

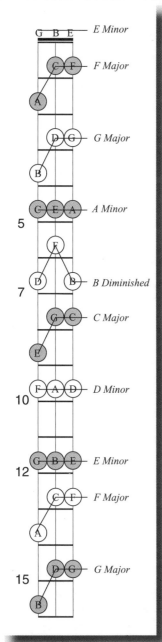

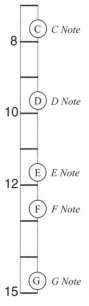

Hello! Welcome to Uncle Tim's Book Of Chords

In 1995 I wrote my first book, Uncle Tim's Building Blocks. That book completely mapped the fretboard for every scale for all 24 major and minor keys. While illustrating the basic theory of diatonic and pentatonic scales, it introduces a simple signature pattern of notes. Uncle Tim's Building Blocks visually illustrates every scale completely without ever violating this signature pattern of notes. It greatly simplifies the process of learning to play scales.

By learning a simple pattern of notes a guitarist can easily have access to every scale, in every key, for the entire fretboard. Visually! Since the guitar repeats every 12 frets, the entire fretboard is completely mapped. Once you understand the 12 fret signature, scales are a breeze.

To me, scales are the basic learning tool we have for understanding the guitar. They are the starting point. Chords are generated from scales and they are the next logical step. Chords are actually built by selecting certain notes in a scale and combining them to form a chord. Since all scales are generated from this signature pattern, and chords are generated from scales, diatonic chords are also generated from inside the twelve fret pattern of notes. This means totally controlling chords is just a few visual steps away.

With a little work, a learning guitarist can use these chords and craft them to create beautiful melodic parts. In 1996 I wrote this book and have since revised it a few times. This book is the companion chord book to Uncle Tim's Building Blocks. It articulates the same visual mapping for chords. This book can be used with Uncle Tim's Building Blocks or alone. It contains everything that must be understood to obtain a complete understanding of diatonic keys. Together with Uncle Tim's Building Blocks, these books provide a visual map of all diatonic basic chords and scales and the theory necessary to breathe life into diatonic keys. By using this book you will understand how it all happens. By playing the exercises and exploring ideas, your musical abilities should explode. As you play these cascades, you may start to generate some ideas of your own. Exploring these ideas is very important.

If you have trouble with the pace of this book , I strongly advise you to consider Uncle Tim's First Year. It can help you gain a basic understanding that can serve as a foundation for this book. I can show you what to do, it is practice that makes it happen. Are you ready to pay some dues?

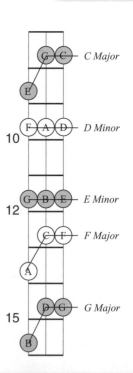

Chords

Chords are three note harmonies that are usually constructed from a key. They are a basic building block for songs. In order to have a chord, you must have at least three notes. The notes are the first or tonic note, the third note and the fifth.

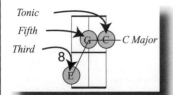

Tonic. This is the note the chord starts on, and usually provides the name for the chord. A C chord starts with the C note. The C note is the tonic note.

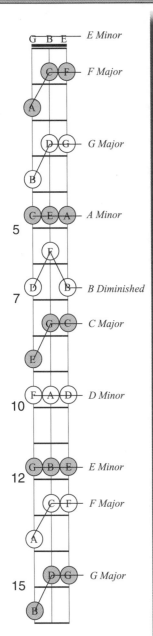

Third. The next note is the third. The third note is the second note in the chord. It is the third note in the major scale. The third note in the C major chord is E. The distance between the C note and the E note is a third. It is three notes apart.

Fifth. The fifth note is the final note in a chord. The fifth is named so because it is the fifth degree of the scale and five degrees away from tonic. Just as the third is named because it is three degrees away from tonic. In this example the G note is the fifth. The distance between the third and the fifth is also a third. It is three notes apart.

Together these three notes (C, E and G) form the C major chord. Anywhere you encounter these three notes, you can combine them to create a C major chord.

All the chords in this diagram relate to each other because they are a family of chords.

The family is C major. These chords are the members of the key of C major. They are built using only the notes of the C major scale. You can use these chords together and create songs in the key of C major. Since they are built on the notes of the scale, they occur in alphabetical order. This particular string of chords starts with the E minor chord. From that point forward the chords will continue right through the seven notes in the key of C major. Notice in the diagram to the left, the chords start with E minor and proceed alphabetically. They are in the key of C major.

On the next few pages we will take a look at chords and how they are created. The chord cascade starts with E minor. E minor is created by using the notes E, G and B. Anytime you use these notes together without any other notes, you are playing an E minor. The next chord is an F major and the following chord is a G major. Then A minor, B diminished, C major and then D minor. **At this point the entire cascade repeats.** Notice the next chord is E minor. And it has the exact same shape as the E minor chord we started with. Only this time it is twelve frets higher.

These Are The Chords Of C Major

When we talk about these chords or the degrees in the scale, you can easily examine them in context using diagrams. You can see how they naturally form inside the key. This can help you form a mental picture of what you hear as you play.

Every twelve frets the guitar repeats.
This entire string of chords above will repeat in order starting at the twelfth fret. The only difference is the new chords will be one octave higher.

Knowing this and being able to use it will drastically cut down what you need to memorize. Anything you learn within the first twelve frets will be applied to the higher frets. There are other relationships we can take use to cut down the memorization even more dramatically. This one eliminates about half the necessary memorization right away.

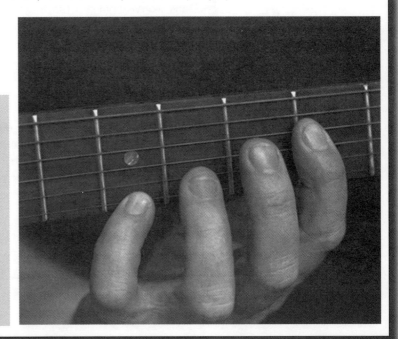

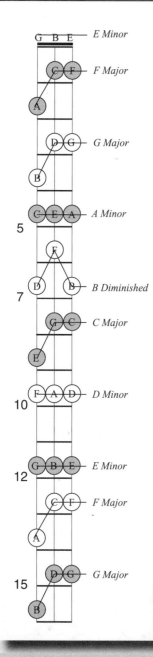

Cascades

As you go down the fretboard towards the bottom of the page, you climb in pitch. So these chords get higher in pitch as they go down the page.

Most musical parts composed on a guitar are either climbing or ascending. You may change the direction at the drop of the hat, but you are either working up or down. Cascades can be a very important tool when constructing musical phrases. They add interest to your creations by allowing you to break away from the standard chords and they provide an excellent avenue for moving around the fretboard. When you practice playing cascades, one of the benefits is you train your ear. You become accustomed to hearing this change in pitch and the full meaning of climbing and descending while playing chords.

Practicing playing chords in cascades will increase your hand strength and your ability to play most any chord form. They are an excellent addition to playing scales.

Triads

Notice these chords are all three note chords. Three notes is the minimum you can use and still construct a chord. If you have only two notes you have an interval. If you have three notes, it qualifies as a chord. Triads are the smallest chord possible.

Triads are three string chords and the most basic available. And all the four, five and six string chords can trace their existence back to simple triads. So these chords are the basic building blocks of all chords. If you are trying to play barre chords and you have trouble holding down the barre, these chords will help develop that skill. Notice there are all sorts of opportunities to play mini-barre chords inside the cascade.

Every String Is A Scale

Take a look at the three strings in the example to the left. The notes on each string are the notes in the key of C major. Each string contains a scale. When we play scales we are using notes individually. When we play chords we are combining notes to create chords. So we are working with three different scale strings to pick out notes to create chords. In this way, you can think of triad cascades as three note scales.

Don't worry about this too much, it is just interesting to know how these chords are generated. It is another good way to visualize the fretboard and incorporate this information with single note lines.

There are only a few different cascades

Here is another very big aid in memorization. Look at the two progressions to the right. The chord forms are identical but the chords are for two different keys. The chords for D major occurred two frets higher. They start on the tenth fret, however, the chords for C major start on the eighth fret. But the form of the chords is the same.

You only need to memorize this sequence of notes once! Each key will use the same sequence of chord forms. Instead of memorizing a different sequence for each key, you only have to memorize it once and apply it to every other key. This eliminates even more memorization. We will make these concepts very clear as we proceed, and you will have many opportunities to gain an understanding and apply them.

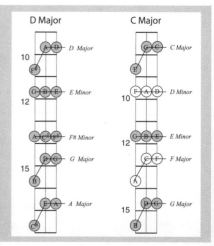

Chord Construction

Chord Types

Did you notice there were three different chord types used on the last page? The three types are:

Major. The major chord occurs three times in a diatonic key. The first or tonic chord and the fourth and fifth chords.

Minor. The minor chord also occurs three times in a diatonic key. The minor chord occupies the second, third and sixth chords. The sixth chord is the relative minor chord, which we will talk about extensively in a few pages.

Diminished. The diminished chord only occurs once in a diatonic key. It is always the chord built on the seventh degree. It is the last chord you encounter before you get to tonic. It is always right next to tonic. Look at the example on the last page to make sure you see this very important relationship.

There is one additional chord form to be aware of. You will not encounter it unless you work with harmonic minor chords. It is called **the augmented chord**. The augmented chord does not appear in standard diatonic keys. Chords are constructed using very specific formulas. The first type of chord we will look at is the major chord. The three components of a chord are the root note, the third and the fifth. The root note is the note the chord is based on. If we are talking about a C major chord, the root note is C. The next note is the third note. The third note determines whether the chord is major or minor. The final note is the fifth note.

Stacking Thirds

Remember when we talked about the third degree being a third away from tonic? The distance from tonic to the third degree is called a third. The distance between the third degree and the fifth degree is also a third. They are both three degrees apart. Chords can be broken into two parts, a lower third and an upper third. Look at the lower third in the major chord below. Notice the first and third are separated by the second degree. Now notice the first and third notes are four frets apart, which is two whole steps. When a third is constructed of two whole steps it is a major third. Notice a whole step is two frets. A half step is the distance you travel when you move one fret. Two whole steps create a major third. The lower third in a major chord is a major third. Now look at the upper third. The upper third is a minor third, it is constructed with a half step and a whole step. This distance is three frets. **The major chord is created by stacking a minor third on top of a major third.** Now look at the minor chord.

The minor chord is created by stacking a major third on top of a minor third. This is just the opposite of the major chord. The placement of the third chord determines whether a chord is major or minor. A chord containing two minor thirds is a diminished chord. And a chord constructed of two major thirds is an augmented third. Take a good look at these diagrams.

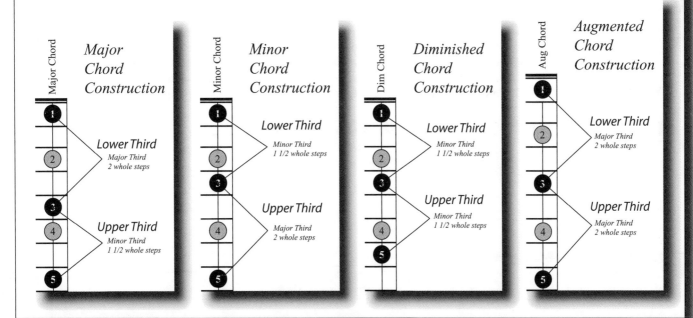

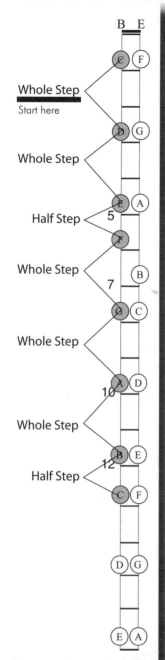

Intervals

The concept of intervals is so fundamental that we are going to look at it in detail. An interval is the distance traveled to sound two notes. This example uses the B and E strings. The B string starts with a B note, one half step below the open B is a C note. The C note is played on the very first fret after the open string. This distance is a half step. On the E string, the very next note is an F, which is one half step below the open E note. Half steps occur between B and C and E and F for the key of C. All the other intervals are whole steps. Examine this graphic until you see this. Then go back to the fretboard graphic and examine this for the entire fretboard. Notice that this is always the same.

Whole Steps	Half Steps
C to D	B to C
D to E	E to F
F to G	
G to A	Half Step = One Fret.
A to B	Whole Step = Two Frets.

Why is this important? The intervals determine the sound of the chord and the scale. In order for a scale to be diatonic, it must adhere to the rule of whole steps and half steps. The distance between the notes in a chord determine if the chord is major, minor, diminished or augmented. Now think about the examples of chord types we just covered and compare them to a C major and D minor chord.

The C chord is made by stacking the 1, 3 and 5 degree of the C scale. C = 1, E = 3 and G = 5. When you combine a first and third degree, you have a third. The distance is referred to as a third, just as the distance between the third and the fifth is a third. You are traveling a third. The distance between C and G is a fifth.

What is the distance between C and E? Look at the graphic and you will see the distance is two whole steps. Between C and D is a whole step, and between D and E is a whole step. When a third is separated by two whole steps, and it is a major third. Now look at E and G on the B string. Between E and F is a half step, between F and G is a whole step. When a third is separated by a half step and a whole step, it is a minor third.

A major chord is constructed by stacking a major then a minor third.
A minor chord is constructed by stacking a minor third and then a major third.
An augmented chord is constructed by stacking two major thirds.
A diminished chord is constructed by stacking two minor thirds.

Does C Major Really Behave According To The Rules?

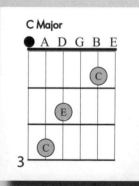

The answer is yes. Even though this chord may not seem like it adheres to the rules of chords, it does. There are only three different notes in this chord. The lowest note in this chord is the C on the A string. The next note is the E on the D string. Then the open string G is next. That is all that is necessary to form this chord and if you add any notes other than these three, it becomes a different chord. However you can add more of the same notes. Notice there are two other notes in this chord. The next note is another C and then an E. That is five notes. Even though there are five notes in this chord and they are spread over more than one octave, this chord still adheres to the rules. Don't be fooled just because the notes are all over the place or not in order.

Describing the twelve keys

Most of the discussion in this book centers around a specific key. Either we are talking about a scale, or some chords, or a song in one key or another. Before we go deep into each key, it will be helpful to realize how the whole thing works.

Diatonic keys are the basis for the music heard in most of the world. Any song heard on the radio today in the western hemisphere will have roots traceable back to a diatonic key. There are twelve major diatonic keys. So there are different letters used to designate the twelve keys. But this system does not use twelve letters, this system is designed to use seven letters. The letters are A, B, C, D, E, F and G. But seven letters is not enough to describe twelve different keys. You can't tell them apart using only seven letters. So the concept of sharps and flats is what extends the system to make it possible to distinguish twelve different keys. When you sharp a note, you move it up one fret. That is described as a sharp. Here is an example. If you move a C note up one fret, it becomes a C# note. It is one fret higher. A flat means to lower the note one fret. If you take that C# note and flatten it, you get a C note.

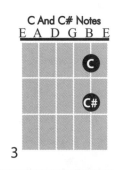

Music works alphabetically

We are talking about sharping and flatting a note and raising the pitch. This occurs in octaves. Octaves are alphabetical. Notes ascend in pitch by climbing through the alphabet. No matter what note you start on, if you climb in pitch you are climbing alphabetically, although you may not stop at every letter.

We Start The Major Keys With C

When we start the actual construction process of diatonic keys we start with C major. Then we proceed either alphabetically or by jumping five degrees to a new key. You can go forward like, C, D, E, F, G, A, B and continue as high as you choose to go. Or you could proceed by moving backwards like C, B, A, G, F, E, D and back to C. Notice this time we started on C and went backwards. You can move in both directions. A guitar has at least three octaves in close reach so you climb through the alphabet three times before you run out of fretboard. Electric guitars have an additional octave available because of the cutaway body. Just remember you can move up or down and you can start on any letter, but when we start to order the keys, we start with C major.

The Twelve Keys

The twelve keys are easily seen on this diagram. To help you visualize this, we are starting with the C note but you could start with any note. And when you climb up in letters, you climb up in pitch. One fret is the smallest movement you can make. We will talk about the spacing and reason some notes have sharps and others don't, but for now we are going to concentrate on the fact, there are twelve notes and twelve keys. The reason there are twelve keys is because the guitar splits the octave into twelve notes (one per fret) and then the sequence repeats again. So there are twelve notes and each note will create a key. We start with the key of C major. We start here because it has no sharps or flats. So if you take this diagram and you remove all the sharps, you will be left with the key of C major, the white notes.

Each Key Is Slightly Different

The first key is C major, no sharps. The next key has one sharp. That is how the first two keys differ. The second key is G major. Were you expecting to go to C#? We are going to jump in five degree increments. Five degrees from C is G. Starting with the keynote and going through the key, the notes are G, A, B, C, D, E, F# and then G again.

The third key has two sharps and the next key after that has three. Each key gets one more sharp and that is how they are different. When you sort these keys based on the order of key construction, you are actually working through the circle of fifths.

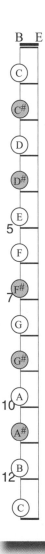

Chart Of Sharps And Flats Of All Diatonic Keys

Key	Relative Minor	Sharps	Flats
C Major	A Minor	None	None
G Major	E Minor	F#	Bbb, Ebb, Abb, Dbb, Gb, Cb, Fb
D Major	B Minor	F#, C#	Bbb, Ebb, Abb, Db, Gb, Cb, Fb
A Major	F# Minor	F#, C#, G#	Bbb, Ebb, Ab, Db, Gb, Cb, Fb
E Major	C# Minor	F#, C#, G#, D#	Bbb, Eb, Ab, Db, Gb, Cb, Fb
B Major	G# Minor	F#, C#, G#, D#, A#	Bb, Eb, Ab, Db, Gb, Cb, Fb
F # Major	D# Minor	F#, C#, G#, D#, A#, E#	Bb, Eb, Ab, Db, Gb, Cb
C # Major	A# Minor	F#, C#, G#, D#, A#, E#, B#	Bb, Eb, Ab, Db, Gb
Ab Major	F Minor	F##, C#, G#, D#, A#, E#, B#	Bb, Eb, Ab, Db
Eb Major	C Minor	F##, C##, G#, D#, A#, E#, B#	Bb, Eb, Ab
Bb Major	G Minor	F##, C##, G##, D#, A#, E#, B#	Bb, Eb
F Major	D Minor	F##, C##, G##, D##, A#, E#, B#	Bb

Start With C Major

Here is a representation of the circle of fifths in a circular diagram. It is shown as a circle to illustrate you can move either forward or backwards. If you wanted to move to the next key forward, you would go to G major. If you wanted to go to the previous key (backwards), you would go to F major. Look at the inside circle. That is the major tonal center. This is the slice of the circle of fifths for C major. This key has no sharps or flats. We are starting on C major.

The Circle Of Fifths

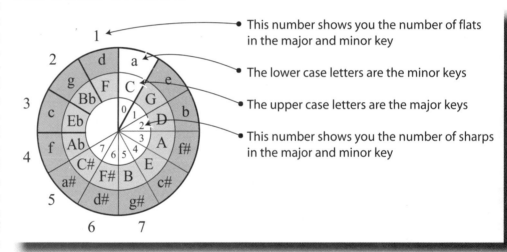

• This number shows you the number of flats in the major and minor key

• The lower case letters are the minor keys

• The upper case letters are the major keys

• This number shows you the number of sharps in the major and minor key

Minor Keys

The lower case letter 'a' is the minor key that is associated with C major. The minor key contains the same notes as the major key. They are related. They are relative to each other. They are identical. They share the same notes and that means they share the same scale and the same chords. A key is defined by the notes in the scale, the key generates the chords native to the key. A minor is the **relative minor** and C major is the **relative major**. Together they make up one slice of the pie. The zero tells you how many sharps are present in the key. In the key of C major, there are no sharps.

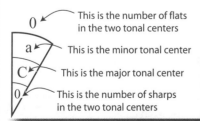

This is the number of flats in the two tonal centers

This is the minor tonal center

This is the major tonal center

This is the number of sharps in the two tonal centers

You can express any key in either sharps or flats (see chart above). If you use the flatted spelling, the numbers on the outside of the circle tell you how many flats are in the key. Notice neither the sharps nor flats go all the way around the circle. Somewhere around C# it becomes difficult to show the sharps on a musical staff, so it is a convenient place to change to the flat spelling. That way it is easier to describe the key. On the real circle of fifths diagram, there is no 0 above C major for the flats. It is not shown.

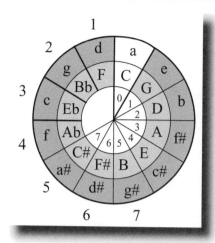

Now that we know how each slice explains a major and a minor key, we can take a look at how each key is positioned in the circle. They don't proceed alphabetically in the circle, yet we know we climb in pitch by working through the alphabet.

The name "Circle of Fifths" gives you a hint. What actually happens is as we go to the next key, we move to the fifth degree in the present key. One fifth away from the present keynote is the next keynote. The distance to the next keynote is a fifth so this is called the circle of fifths.

The Fifth Degree Of C Major Is G

G is the next key! We form a new key on the G note. Now we construct G major the same way we did C major. The spacing of the notes stays the same from key to key. Now we start at the keynote and add the notes of the key. G is the first note of the key. When we get to the F note, we sharp it. That means when we play this note we move it up one fret, which raises the note. The fifth degree of G Major is D. So D major becomes the next key in the circle of fifths. It also adds one additional sharp.

Working Forward

In the example below and to the right, notice F major is the first example. Remember you can move either forward or backwards. From C you can go backwards to F, or forward to G. The keys of G and F are going to be very similar to C major. This is an important concept to understand. The circle of fifths is circular because you can move both forward and backwards and keys to each side are similar.

Working Backwards

If you travel backwards, remember to go five degrees backwards to locate the last key. Start with the right hand keynote and moves back five degrees to F.

This concept is illustrated in the bottom diagram. Five degrees behind C is F. Five degrees in front of C is G.

Either way you go, you move in five degree increments each time you move.

When we get into each key we will look at this concept in detail. By the time we move through three or four keys, you will have a working understanding of this concept.

This is the basis of the circle of fifths.

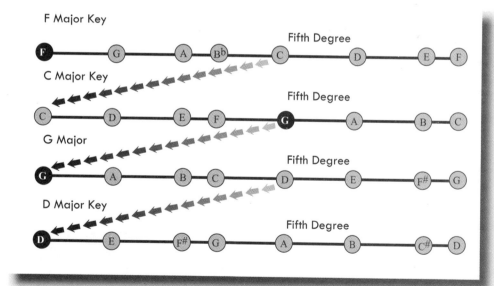

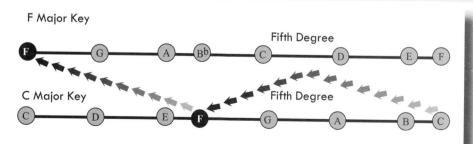

Triads Based On A Major Scale

As discussed earlier, we can build a C major scale by starting with C and adding D, E, F, G, A, B, and then C. A two-octave scale would look like this.

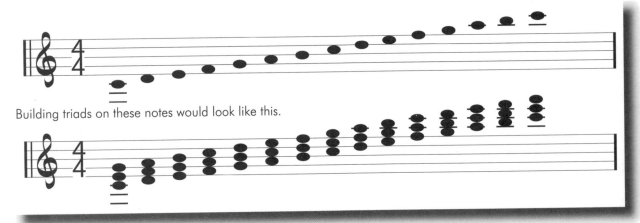

Building triads on these notes would look like this.

Now we must examine each of these triads to determine which ones are major and which ones are minor triads. Fortunately, all major scales create chords that adhere to the same rule. Learn it once and it is applicable to all keys.

Triads Based On The Major Key

The diagram below is a representation of the key of C major, laid out so you can see how each of the chords in the key is constructed. Remember chords are always constructed from bottom to top, lower third first, and then the upper third. In a C chord, the lower third is C to E and the upper third is E to G. A major and minor third together will create a perfect fifth. Two minor thirds form a diminished fifth. Notice all the chords below are perfect fifths except for the seventh chord which is a diminished or imperfect fifth.

Do you see that the third degree determines if a chord is a major or minor chord? Also make sure you notice a perfect fifth is constructed by combining a minor and a major third in any order. Did you notice that an augmented chord has not been discussed? That type of a chord will appear in the harmonic form of the relative minor key.

Chord	C	D	E	F	G	A	B	C
Degree	1	2	3	4	5	6	7	1
Triad	Maj	min	min	Maj	Maj	min	Dim	Maj
Lower Third	M	m	m	M	M	m	m	M
Upper Third	m	M	M	m	m	M	m	m

The tonic note of the chord

One half step from the tonic note

One whole step from the tonic note

A minor third (shown in gray)

A major third (shown in gray)

A fourth (shown in white)

A diminished fifth degree (shown in gray)

A perfect fifth degree (shown in gray)

The C Major / A Minor Scale

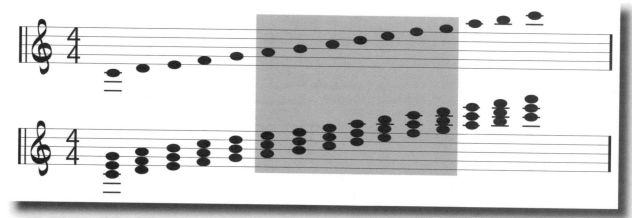

The relative minor has a very close tie with the related major key. They share all the same notes and they use the same scale. As you can see from the notation above, they also share the same chords. This notation illustrates that the relative minor is an extension of the major scale. Do you see that we can continue notating the major scale to include the relative minor scale (gray box)? The relative minor of C major is A minor. A minor uses the very same scale and chords. You would describe the scale by including A, B, C, D, E, F and G. There are no sharps or flats in either the key of C major or A minor. They are the exact same, only the starting note is different.

However, all minor keys have three different forms. Each of these forms is different from the previous form by the addition of a sharp to a specific note. The three different forms are A minor, A minor harmonic and A minor melodic. The A minor harmonic form has typically been used in chord construction to specifically alter the relationships between intervals. For the major and relative minor scale, the same chords structures are used. The progression is major, minor, minor, major, major, minor and dim (if we are talking in relative major terms). If we construct the chords for the minor key using the harmonic minor form, we will introduce an additional sharp and therefore construct different chords. This will alter the sequence of major, minor and diminished triads. It will introduce an augmented triad. You will see this on the next page, but first we will describe the harmonic and melodic forms in musical notation.

The A Minor Harmonic Minor Scale

The A Minor Melodic Minor Scale

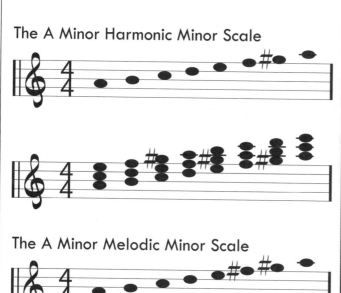

The A minor harmonic form differs from the A minor scale by adding a sharp to the seventh degree (the G note). Every time the G note is used it will be sharped. This will affect three chords within the scale. That will in turn change the type of chords that are formed. The harmonic form has a different chord sequence for the major, minor and diminished forms.

The A minor melodic form differs from the A minor scale by adding a sharp to the sixth and seventh degree. Every time the F and G notes are used ascending the scale, they will be sharped. When the scale is played descending, the sharps are dropped and the natural notes are played.

Another way to eliminate memorization

The related major and minor keys share the identical family of notes and chords. When you memorize the major key, you automatically memorize the related minor key. As you use it, you will understand this.

The Three Forms Of The Minor Scale

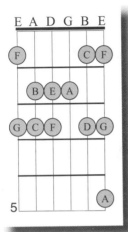

A Minor Scale

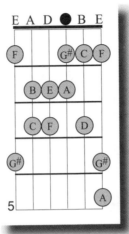

A Minor Harmonic Scale

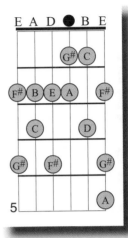

A Minor Melodic Scale

Altering The Relative Minor Scale

In the harmonic and melodic versions, the relative minor scale is altered. Why has this complication been added and how does it affect the sound of the scale and chords?

There are many reasons why this was done, but a main reason was to change the sound of the scale and the sound of the chords based on the scale. In the harmonic version, the seventh degree of the scale has been sharped, providing for a stronger and closer relationship with the tonic note. By sharping the seventh degree, it intensifies the feeling of movement to the tonic note. In other words, it increases the need to resolve the sound by reaching tonic. In the harmonic minor form, the relationship between the seventh degree and tonic is just like the major key. If you play the harmonic minor scale, you may see that it does intensify the need to sound the tonic note.

The Practical Application

The minor key can be used when constructing a song by itself or as a bridge to another progression from the related key. Of course, there are many different things you can do with the key. When playing in the related major key, you can transfer to the relative minor key in a transparent way. If you stay strictly in the natural form, you may not notice a difference, especially when constructing lead lines. However, if you use the harmonic form of the key, you may notice a difference right away. After all you are now playing a G#. To a trained ear it will become obvious that the note is sharp and certainly different. Play each of the scales and see if your ear can tell the difference between forms.

Notice that in the harmonic form, the distance between F and G# is three frets. When you are playing in an unaltered major or minor key, you will never go a distance greater than two frets before sounding the next note. In this way the signature of notes gives its identity away at a glance.

Soloing Using The Melodic Scale

You might wonder about playing the F# and G# only when ascending while using the melodic minor scale. Once you become familiar with the sound of the scale, you can make up your own mind and use the sharps only while ascending or maybe even on occasion while descending. After all it's your solo! This may never become an issue unless you are playing in a style that relies on it such as one of the many forms of jazz.

Chord Construction For The Relative Minor

Here is a chart of the key of C extended to include the A minor scale.

A Minor Scale

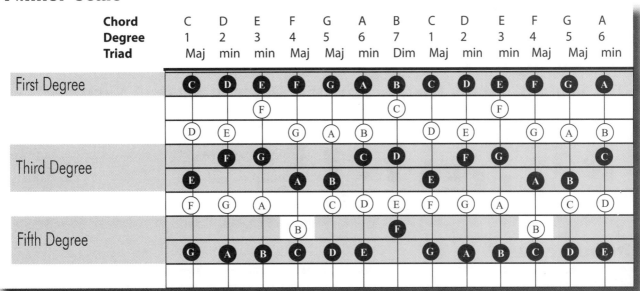

Chord	C	D	E	F	G	A	B	C	D	E	F	G	A
Degree	1	2	3	4	5	6	7	1	2	3	4	5	6
Triad	Maj	min	min	Maj	Maj	min	Dim	Maj	min	min	Maj	Maj	min

The A Minor Harmonic Scale

Chord	C	D	E	F	G#	A	B	C	D	E	F	G#	A
Degree	3	4	5	6	7	1	2	3	4	5	6	7	1
Triad	Aug	min	Maj	Maj	Dim	min	Dim	Aug	min	Maj	Maj	Dim	min

Understanding Intervals

This chart graphically shows an octave of the A minor harmonic form.

When the added sharp of the G(#) note falls on the first, third or fifth degree, it will alter the third and change the type of chord formed as shown.

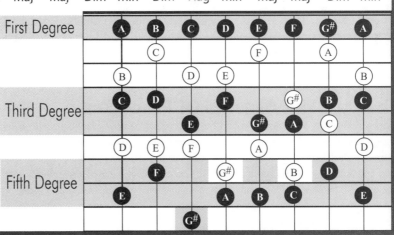

Notice that changing the seventh degree of the A minor scale affects three different chords in the scale. The first chord affected is the third chord. Instead of being a major chord, it is now an augmented chord. The fifth note is sharped and the chord is now constructed of two major thirds. Notice that the G is not a perfect fifth anymore. The D minor chord does not contains a G#, and therefore is not an issue. The lower third for the E chord has changed to become a major third that will change the chord to a major chord. The F chord does not contain a G#, and therefore is not affected. Remember that even though the chart shows intervals 1 through 5, only the 1, 3 and 5 are considered (shaded notes). If the first, third or fifth degree is not affected, the chord will not change.

The chord formed on the seventh degree of the minor scale is now a diminished chord. The chord is now constructed of two minor thirds, and therefore becomes a diminished chord. Do you see how adding a sharp and changing the scale has resulted in altering the type of chords constructed? If you see a minor chord progression that proceeds, minor, dim, aug,

The Scale Of C Major In Musical Notation

The Scale Of Triads For The Key Of C Major In Musical Notation

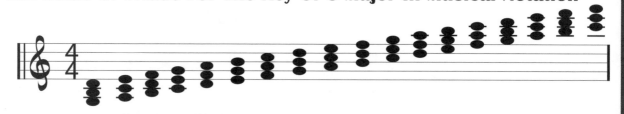

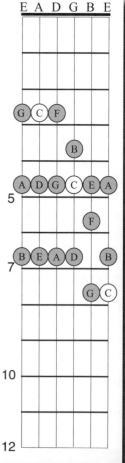

Why Do We Care?

There are several good reasons. Have you ever strummed a chord and wondered if you could construct a song with that chord or if there were other chords that naturally work with it? Have you ever wondered how a guitar is set up or how it works? If you understand how the guitar works and the logical progression of music, it will add more enjoyment when you play. It will also increase your playing options. In a short amount of time you will begin to take advantage of this information and it will show up in your work.

Knowing the notes of the fretboard makes it easier to change to a different key. Knowing the notes of each scale will complete your understanding of keys. Once you understand keys, you have access to the complete palette. At first this seems daunting. After all, there are a lot of scales, chords and notes and learning them all would take an incredible investment of time and memorization. By using the visual pattern as a road map and taking advantage of the repetitive nature of the fretboard, we can make the task much easier.

What Are The Benefits Of Practicing?

If you have made a commitment to the guitar, practice will fulfill your dreams for the instrument! A serious commitment for me means I realize I will play the guitar for the rest of my life. That does not mean that I practice the same amount every week or that I am always knocking myself out to learn something. Since I have made the commitment, I continue to learn and use some ideas more than others. Their revelance may not be easily seen at first, but I keep working with new information and eventually make good use of it.

When you learn something that is not easily applied, it can be difficult to understand the value of that information. If you continue to work with it as you can, you mentally continue to fit the information into place. Your mind will work the information in a subconscious way. If I am going to learn something difficult, I try to read the information once a day or so before I really try to use it. This allows me to have the general concepts in my head before I have to manipulate them. It is not as foreign to me and therefore I have a little head start. This allows me to learn a little faster and keep the frustration level down.

How to proceed

Read this in a relaxed environment so you can think about the information and visualize the concepts and take your time. Afterwards, when you approach the guitar you might start to experiment with new ideas. With consistent practice, those ideas are turned into music, and your personal style can emerge or take on a new facet.

How To Practice And What To Expect!

I break my musical study into three parts. They are scales, chords and songs.

I start out my day with a session of scales. If possible I always start with diatonic scales, three notes per string, six strings, two octave runs that stretch my fingers individually. I also play pentatonic and other kinds of scales, but diatonic scales are the most important ones and should be your starting point.

Scales will help your fingers master the physical movements necessary to play music. Your fingers will be much stronger if you include scales in your daily workout. If you practice for three hours a day, make one of them scales. One of the reasons many guitarists do not play scales is because they do not understand the benefits.

What are the benefits of playing scales? They are numerous. First as mentioned, scales will strengthen your hand and provide an understanding of the fretboard. Scales will help you to travel over the entire fretboard and develop an understanding of the tonal quality of each string up and down the neck. The coordination of your right and left hands will increase rapidly.

Another benefit is understanding the available tools for musical improvisation and construction. To improvise over a random piece of music requires that you know a little about choices for movement. Scales contain all the notes in any given key. If you want to know what notes are available for formation of lead lines, chords, arpeggios and special effects, the scale will contain them and only them.

Another important benefit comes with the passage of time. Playing scales will continue to make you feel more comfortable with the fretboard. In time it will become very comfortable. Increasing your hand strength while polishing the pathways for movement on a guitar will make you a better player capable of many moves. There are times when the practice you put in two weeks earlier will show up in a very unexpected way. You may not anticipate it, but it will show up. You will play things that you did not know you could. It is a very pleasant surprise and it continues to happen time after time, if you play scales!

Chords are the second part of the practice schedule. The second hour is given to playing chords. It is essential that you revisit chords on a regular basis if you wish to use them on demand. Chords will exercise your hands in a different way than scales. You generally play more than one note at a time with chords. Chords are similar to scales but now you are playing specific notes of a scale. Also, the right or picking hand will get a different workout. Rather than a linear picking of the string, you can strum, finger pick or flat pick. Practicing chords in the sequence of the scale will give you a sense of the appropriateness of each chord in relation to another. This can shape your ability to write a song in the framework of a key. It can also increase your ability to have the right chord at the right time.

There are two ways I go about practicing chords in relation to one another. The first is to start (in the key of C) with a C chord and then play the D minor, E minor, F major, G major and A minor. With the exception of the B diminished chord, I have played through the scale of chords for C major. These are typical chords that you see every guitarist use at three different spots on the neck. I break these sections into the open string position, the middle position (encompassing roughly the third to seventh frets) and the third position which is usually near the 12th fret. You can play every chord within any four frets, so the next higher or lower octave of a chord is usually no more than four frets higher or lower.

Playing triads is the second way. This means playing the 1, 3 and 5 notes only. Start on the lowest three strings and play seven chords until you reach an octave. Move to the next set and play the next seven chords. Move up one set, and then move up again. You will see examples of this very shortly. Triads are very important to know and can generate creativity. By learning triads for the guitar, your choice of things to play will immediately increase. Sometimes I will work out by selecting a set of chords in a triad cascade and focus on them. There are many different ways of practicing.

Songs are the reason we play chords and scales. Scales and chords comprise (most of) the technical skills you will develop. Songs express the creative or artistic skills you develop. **Before any artistic skills can emerge, at least some technical skills must be present.** The songs you pick to play will be according to your individual interests. Combined with your technical skills, your individual style will emerge.

Moving Up The Fretboard One Fret At A Time

When you work through the Circle of Fifths, you are jumping five degrees at a time. Between C and G the physical distance is seven frets. It can be difficult to visualize the distance and the movement of the pattern in seven-fret, five-degree jumps. It can be much easier to compare the keys of C and C# graphically. Why? Because they are separated by only one fret. If you move the pattern up one fret, it becomes a C#. This is remarkable, because the Key of C# has seven sharps while the key of C has none, and all we are doing is moving the pattern one fret higher to become the key of C#.

By moving the entire pattern up one fret, you are now playing in a different key. All the same relationships are intact and the pattern of notes compensated for the sharps or flats in the new key. The relationship of whole step, whole step, half step, whole step, whole step, whole step, half step is maintained. It must be or it does not qualify as a diatonic key! This is the theory of music explained for the guitar. This is not a short cut or a gimmick to be forgotten later. This is how the diatonic keys work! You will see this as we go along.

Enharmonic Spellings

An enharmonic spelling is another musical way of saying the same thing. On the last page we discussed an F## and a G. We saw that they are in fact the same note. If I asked you to play an F##, you would play a G note. You may choose to call it an F##, as we do with scales in certain keys, but whatever you call it, the note is the same.

We use a certain enharmonic spelling because it is the easiest way to describe a key. When you look at the key of F, you could say the key of F contains F##, C##, G##, D##, A#, E# and B# or you could say it contains Bb. You can easily see this on a musical staff.

Here is an exercise to illustrate that these two spellings are the same thing.

Key	Degree 1	2	3	4	5	6	7	1
E#	E#	F##	G##	A#	B#	C##	D##	E#
F	F	G	A	Bb	C	D	E	F

Do you see that you could spell the same scale two different ways? It is so much easier to spell it as an F. If you do not understand this, go to the Key of F and change the spellings of the notes on the fretboard so that they match the exercise above.

Enharmonic Spelling Of F Major

These staffs indicate the exact same thing. The number of sharps and double sharps present can only indicate the key of F major or E# major.

It is much easier to flip the spelling which signifies the key of F major by using only one flat. You do not have to look hard at the key signature to recognize this as the key of F major.

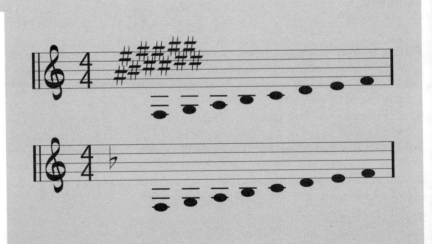

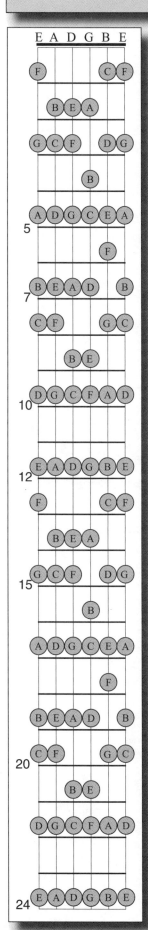

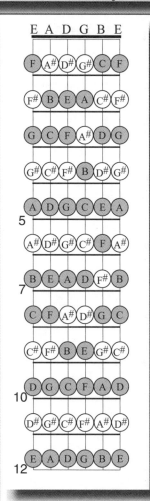

The Practical Application Of Construction

There are twelve possible notes on a guitar. No matter where you look, you will find only twelve different notes available. After you encounter twelve notes on any string, the sequence of notes begins to repeat.

But diatonic keys do not use all twelve notes. A diatonic key only uses seven notes. The key of C has seven notes in it, just like all the other diatonic keys do. A diatonic key splits the twelve chromatic notes into seven positions. **These seven notes are always the same distance apart.** The right hand diagram shows all the notes on the guitar. This is the chromatic scale.

The diagram to the left illustrates the twelve fret signature of notes for C major. This is the only pattern you must memorize. Every key will use this pattern of notes. The only difference is where you barre it. We introduce it first for C major and then we apply it to all the other keys.

These notes are all the notes of the key of C on a fretboard. Notice at the 12th fret, the strings repeats themselves. We have traveled from E through F, G, A, B, C and D until we arrived at E again. From here the process repeats again. Every string does the same thing. The A string starts with A and travels the sequence of notes until A again appears at the 12th fret. The other strings do the same exact thing. What you learn below the 12th fret will be identical to the same position above the 12th fret. Learn it for the first twelve frets and know it for frets 13 through 24.

Everything in the Key of C is present in this pattern! Every chord that is built in the key of C is present in this pattern, and every scale passage is here as well. When you can play the chords built on the key of C, you can transfer those exact same chords to any key. They will always be in the exact same order with the exact same fingerings.

By concentrating on the degrees of the scales instead of the notes, it is easier to understand the relationships. The chords will proceed in an orderly fashion one through seven and then repeat.

Songs In The Key Of C

Any song or sets of chords that you can use to create songs in the key of C are in this signature pattern. If you want to add notes between chords to a progression, you can choose any of these notes. If you want to make up a chord, you can use these notes to experiment with.

If you want to create a lead over some chords, use any of these notes and they will sound right and be in the correct key. These are just a few of the practical applications available. There are many, many more ways to use this information, but you may not see or understand them yet!

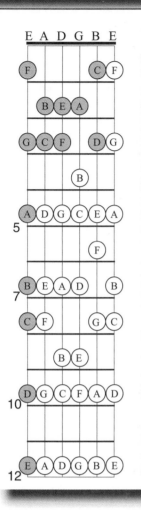

Alternate Pathways on a Fretboard

The gray circles represent notes that can be used to complete the scale of C. Notice that by going up the string or from left to right, the same notes are used, and not only the same notes, but the same pitch. The sound of the notes is identical. The A note on the fifth fret of the low E string is the same note as the open A string. This is a key concept, because travel to and from higher notes can be accomplished by going up or across strings. To travel to lower registers in the key, go down the string or across to the left. Remember we are climbing up the scale of C. Pick a note and start to ascend alphabetically.

Look at the E string to the right-hand side. This is called the high E string. The string is tuned to an E note. This E is two octaves higher than the lowest note on the fretboard, the low open E string. The first octave ends on the E note located on the second fret of the D string. This note is also the beginning of the second octave. Do you see that the shaded dots in the first three frets are a two octave scale run in the key of C?

A Two Octave Scale

Here is a graphic to help you understand a two octave scale. The first octave is in the white dots, beginning with an open E string through the second E note on the D string. The second octave begins on that E and continues through the gray dots and to the open E note on the E string. The black dots would represent the F and G notes of the next octave. Also notice that the E on the D string is the exact same note as the E on the 12th fret of the low E string.

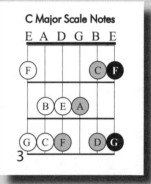

C Major Scale Notes

Describing The Scale With Musical Notation

The notes below describe the first octave. Either pathway described above can be used to play this progression of notes. Notation will tell you what notes to play, but you must decide exactly where to play the notes. This information should start you thinking about pathways for traveling on the fretboard.

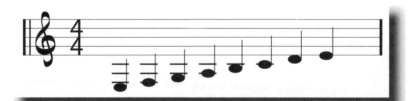

Breathing Life Into Your Base Of Knowledge

Next time you go to see a performer, look closely. A good guitarist will usually move to different parts of the fretboard. Along the way and in between chords you may see the use of some accent notes. Often you see chords you know but slightly different than the way you might play them. All of these tricks are designed to take the fundamental information and cloak or change it. They are all implementations of the creative process and defining aspects of individual styles. You start with basic concepts and you twist it to some new shape!

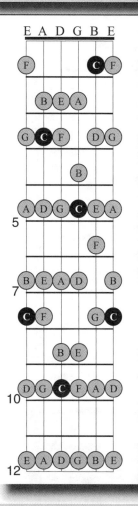

The Diatonic Pattern

This is the physical pattern that every major and unaltered minor scale will use. On a fretboard, everything is movable. Remember the diatonic signature is created by starting on any note and spacing notes as per the whole step, whole step, half step, whole step, whole step, whole step, half step rule. If you start on the keynote (C in this example) on any string and you place the notes in the key using the spacing just mentioned, you will create this pattern.

Notice this pattern maps only the notes in the key of C. Notice twelve frets above the E note on the low E string is another E. Same for the high E string. Actually the note each string is tuned to will occur on the twelfth fret. Everything will repeat at the twelfth fret! This entire signature will repeat at the twelfth fret! Read the next paragraph carefully.

That means this twelve fret signature is all we have to memorize. Remember each key is going to use this exact same information (which you will see shortly). The names of the notes are going to change but this pattern and the spacing of notes will stay exactly the same. They must because the rules of diatonic keys dictate it. This is all you have to memorize!

The black dots are the location of all the keynotes. As we look at each key you may notice this pattern is moved up or down the fretboard so the black dot falls on the keynote. There are two main concepts on this page to notice. First, this pattern contains all the chords and scales for a key, so we will need to know this pattern in great detail. Second, every key will use the exact same pattern. Once you know the pattern in great detail, we can explore all the other keys quite easily.

This is a huge concept and will take a little time to really understand and use. The following pages are going to describe each key using the same pattern. We use this information to describe everything from the big picture to the smallest detail and any details you may know already, are in it too.

Identifying The First Tonic Chord

This is the same pattern as the one above. However, this time we are highlighting one chord in particular. This barre chord can be any major chord if it is moved to the right position. At this location it is a C major chord. Move it up one fret and it becomes a C# major chord. Move it two frets higher and it becomes a D major chord. We are going to use this chord as a marker in the twelve fret pattern to mark the same tonic chord form for each key.

Every key will use this pattern and this chord form will be the tonic chord in each key. This is one chord in a chain of chords that are present in this pattern of notes. As you see each key and this chord form, keep in mind that the entire chain of chords will also be present for every new key. Everything is present and shifted to a new key. You may need to reread these pages several times after you see the following pages.

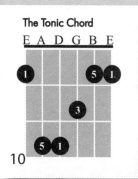

The Tonic Chord

Make sure that you recognize this chord in the pattern as you look at the next few pages. As you examine material in this way it is common to see bits and pieces of information you already know show up. It is a sign you are starting to connect things. Take time to examine any relationships that you notice. This can cause major pieces to fall into place. Remember it's all here.

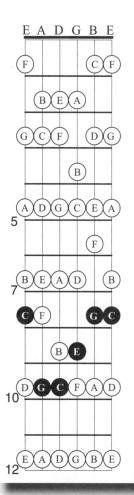

The 2 Diatonic Keys

C Scale

C# Scale

D Scale

D# Scale

E Scale

F Scale

The Physical Signature Of All Twelve Keys

You should probably look at this page while holding it about three feet from your face. Look at this information as a whole pattern. The twelve fret pattern is within the diagram shown here. Do you see that it is the very same pattern for every key! This exercise moves the pattern up a half step to form a new key. Looking at it in this visual way helps you to understand the gradual change as the pattern is moved up the smallest increment (one fret).

Remember the tonic chord shown on the last page. Here it is in each key (in white dots). It is the same chord form occurring in the same place within the twelve fret signature. For each new key it is properly positioned to be the tonic chord. Also notice that each key adheres to the whole step, whole step, half step, whole step, whole step, whole step, half step rule.

Did you notice that there are 12 examples here? 12 frets to consider, 12 notes, one key for each note. Did you also realize that there are 12 spots on the Circle of Fifths? To repeat the sequence of notes, we only need to cover 12 frets. Notice each of the fretboards above is 24 frets long. The pattern is shown repeating once for every key.

Now we will break down this twelve fret signature and examine the chords contained within. As we study each key, it will reinforce the others. All this information is the same for each key. The only thing that is different is the location. If you know the scales for each key, you already have an advantage. We will use them to build chords.

The 12 Diatonic Keys

F# Scale	G Scale	G# Scale	A Scale	A# Scale	B Scale

The Other Chords

We have mapped the one tonic chord (as shown in this example). I have implied there are other chords in this pattern. Since this is a map of the keys, it makes sense that everything for the key is contained in this pattern. It is! However, there are exceptions! In this pattern is every chord, one through seven, and several variations of every chord. Not only will you find the common chords that we work with every day, but you will also find complete sets of triads.

As we discussed before, triads are three-note chords containing the first, third and fifth degrees of a scale starting on the note of the chord. Every note of the scale will produce a triad. In fact, it will produce at least three versions of a triad. This will be explained in a few pages when we discuss inversions.

This pattern contains full scales of triads for all inversions. In a moment we will explore them. Triads are extremely powerful tools in the creation of music. If you practice them, they will show up in your music. Triads have the power to give you several choices for any chord that you will ever play. They can be used to create secondary parts to a composition that can accent and fill in as needed. By studying triads, you will greatly expand your musical limits. Inside this 12 fret pattern are also four, five and six string chords. Remember back to Chords In The Key Of C presented earlier? All you have to do to create a chord is to identify the three notes that make up the chord. Then draw lines between the notes so the chord is easily identified.

We will start with the four, five and six string chords on the very next page and then move to the triads. Remember these examples will show the chords built on each degree for the key of C. We are using the key of C as an example. In the second half of the book we will look at each key.

The Pattern Repeats Every Twelve Frets

The repetition of the fretboard is so important we are going to spend a little more time looking at this concept. No matter which note you pick, the exact same note will show up twelve frets higher. Also notice the tonic chord highlighted on the last page repeats twelve frets higher. Remember everything on a guitar repeats every twelve frets. If you have used **Uncle Tim's Building Blocks** you have used this same signature to build scales. The chords we are going to explore in each key are companion chords to those scales. They are meant to be used together.

Picking Chords Out Of The Pattern

Since we are using only the notes in the key of C, and all the chords in the key of C are built using only the notes of the key of C, it stands to reason that all the chords in the key of C are right here in this pattern. They are! Not only are they all here but they are tightly packed in, one right after another. The example to the right shows how each succeeding note is used to build chords.

Cascading Chords

We are connecting these chords by drawing lines between the notes. You have already seen how to create chords in the key of C. Let's apply that information and create these chords. Notice that all notes are used. Also notice that the chords automatically fall into place with the rules governing major and minor chords. Also notice that this example uses two barre chord forms. The two forms repeat within the pattern. If you wanted to, you could continue to connect the dots and create the chords for the rest of the key. Actually in a few pages we are going to do just that! These chords occur one after another, they cascade up and down the fretboard. Many other chords are here too and they all work together.

As you see this twelve fret pattern moved to a new location, remember these chords are still packed in there and now take on the names of the chords in the new key. The forms will stay the same for each degree. This will hold true for all keys. By practicing the flow of these chords you are preparing to play in any key.

Repeatable Chord Forms

These are the forms that are used in the example to the right. The major chord form is the same form used by the tonic chord on the last page. Notice these chords use all six strings. You can move these chords to new positions and they will always be major and minor chords respectively. These forms are easily moved because all the strings are played. Everything gets moved up together. This page illustrates that the guitar repeats on a variety of levels.

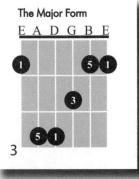

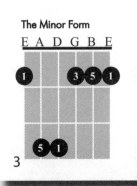

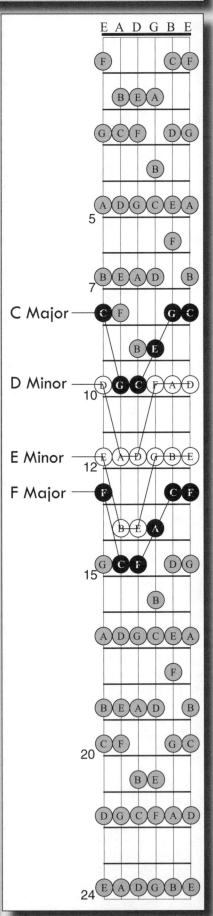

A Major Open String Chord

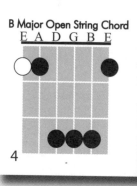

B Major Open String Chord

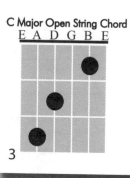

C Major Open String Chord

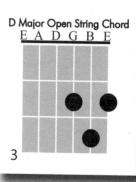

D Major Open String Chord

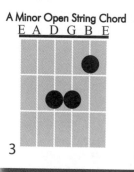

A Minor Open String Chord

B Minor Open String Chord

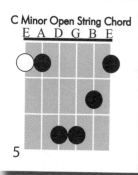

C Minor Open String Chord

D Minor Open String Chord

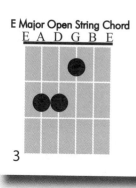

E Major Open String Chord

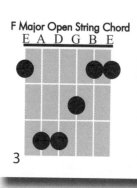

F Major Open String Chord

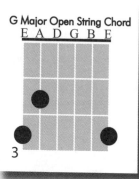

G Major Open String Chord

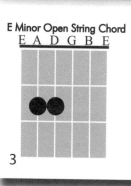

E Minor Open String Chord

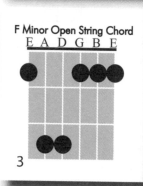

F Minor Open String Chord

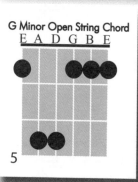

G Minor Open String Chord

Building Repeatable Chord Forms

Start with the open-string A major chord and look at the differences between the major and minor form. Do you see that the A minor is the same as the A major chord except the third is lowered to make the chord minor? Also notice that some chords do not use open strings! These chords do not contain the open-string notes or they are not convenient. Another item to notice is some chords are forms of chords that occur lower on the fretboard and are now repeated at higher frets. An example is the F minor and G minor chords.

Altering The Form

Some chord forms will be altered as they are played. A good example is the D major form shown on this page. As you look at the next page, you will notice that the D major is played like the open string C. Move the C chord out of the open strings to see what I mean. Remember to barre the open strings as the form is moved.

C Major / D Minor Form

The open-string C major chord and the D minor chord are the basis for this progression. Notice the progression of major, minor, minor, major, major, minor and dim. Make sure you recognize this as the diatonic sequence for progressing through a key.

If you move the pattern to another position, you can still use these chords, just move them with the pattern and apply them to the new key. Notice all major chords are the same as are all the minor chords.

Building Barre Chords

Start with the open-string C major chord and the open string D minor chord. These two forms will be repeated in the proper sequence through the sixth degree. After the diminished chord (seventh degree), the sequence repeats itself. Look for the C chord at the 13th fret. Do not forget to play the G and E on the 12th fret. They were played as open strings at the nut. You can play any of these chords at any fret. However, to form a chord that is contained within the key you must use them at these locations.

Remember for the key of C, the chords in the key are C major, D minor, E minor, F major, G major, A minor and B diminished. If you move this entire pattern up one fret, the same forms apply but the chords are now C# major, D# minor, E# minor, F# major, G# major, A# minor, and B# diminished. By moving the pattern up one fret, you are changing the key to C#. You can jump ahead to that key and check if you like.

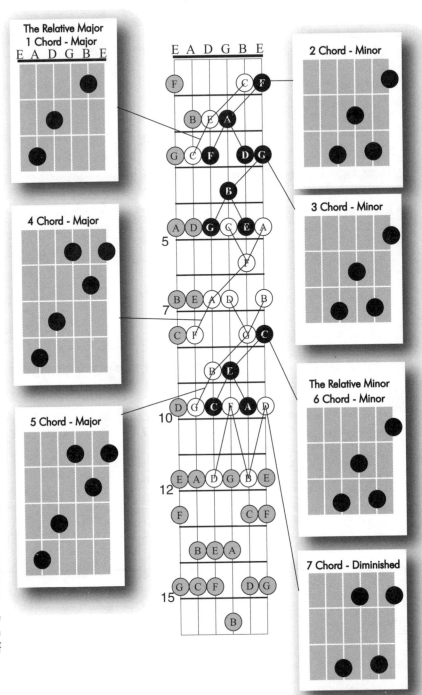

The Relative Major
1 Chord - Major

2 Chord - Minor

3 Chord - Minor

4 Chord - Major

5 Chord - Major

The Relative Minor
6 Chord - Minor

7 Chord - Diminished

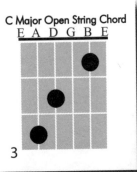

C Major Open String Chord

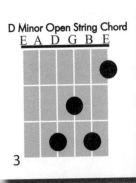

D Minor Open String Chord

Forms

These are the chord formss in this cascade. Each one is used for all the major chords or minor chords. So in this example there are only three chord forms. The major, minor and diminished chord forms.

The next examples will do the same thing. So each key will use all these chord forms to create chords in each key.

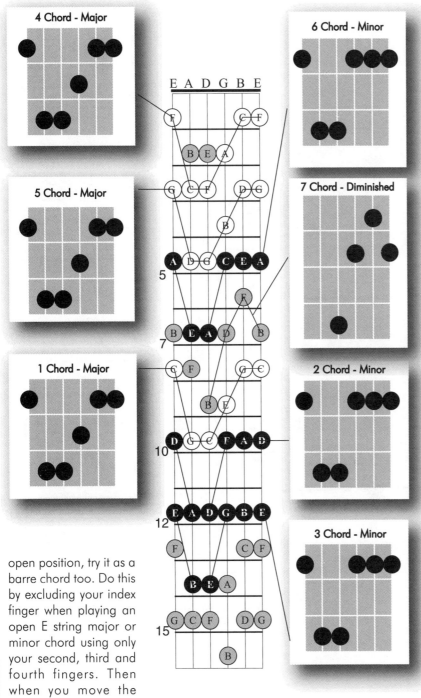

4 Chord - Major

5 Chord - Major

1 Chord - Major

6 Chord - Minor

7 Chord - Diminished

2 Chord - Minor

3 Chord - Minor

E Major / Minor Form

The open string E chord is quite movable. By barring the notes usually played by the open strings, this form can travel up or down the fretboard. The E minor form barre chord is very similar and quite useful. With time this example, and the applications for it will become very important. These chord forms will show up in lots of songs. Remember all the major chords share the same form as do the minor chords. The diminished is always an oddball form.

Every Scale
Contains Chords

Here are some common everyday chords that are used in this example. They are not limited to what we will see here and they occur in many different forms. This particular form starts with the open E major chord. The E major chord is played with three open strings, the E strings and the B string. As you move the chord away from the nut of the neck, you must now play the open strings by barring notes. Most of the time they are arranged so this can be done by barring strings with the index finger. If you have played the E minor chord in the

open position, try it as a barre chord too. Do this by excluding your index finger when playing an open E string major or minor chord using only your second, third and fourth fingers. Then when you move the chord up, use your index finger as a barre. This minor chord also creates a minor barre chord. As you work up the scale, you use major and minor chord forms to play the correct chord for the degree. Remember it's:

1	2	3	4	5	6	7
Major	Minor	Minor	Major	Major	Minor	Dim

This will hold true for each of these forms. Check and make sure.

E Major Open String Chord
E A D G B E

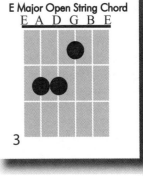

3

A Fifth In A Barre Chord
E A D G B E

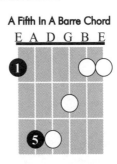

E Minor Open String Chord
E A D G B E

3

A Major / Minor Form

The open string A minor and A major chords are the basis for this progression. Notice the sixth chord is the open string A minor chord. The tonic chord is the played three frets higher than the open-string (sixth) A minor chord.

Repeatable Barre Chords

Here is another example of progressions within the diatonic pattern. As you are playing these chords, remember that the entire scale of C is available to add runs, lead lines or a combination of notes for special interest. Composing a second part over a rhythm track using this information can provide considerable ideas for experimentation.

As you will see in a few pages, there are many different forms in many different positions. Using them with each other reinforces their relationship to one another and makes it easier to find and use them during an improvisation. Combining four, five and six-string chords with triads can introduce avenues for travel and full-bodied sound. Combining the two types of chords with scale passages can provide access to all points of the guitar in whatever form you choose.

Fifths

Rock and roll uses the one and five intervals for much of the rhythm. A fifth is played using the first degree with the fifth degree. Notice that a fifth is present in this barre chord below (black dots). In rock, this type of chord is the basis for a large percentage of songs. It also occurs in barre chords shown on the previous page.

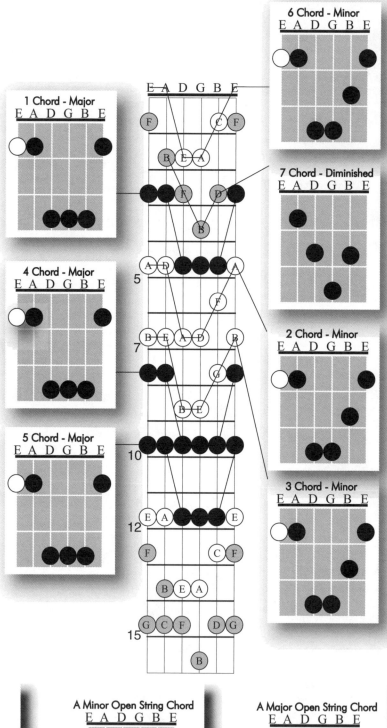

The Ordering Of Notes In A Triad

What determines the order of notes in a chord? Triads usually have three notes, the first degree, the third degree and the fifth degree, but the ordering of the notes can vary. If you construct triads based on the following formula you will be in one of the three primary inversions. Inversions will arrange the notes and change the sound of the chord. Remember the notes present will determine the name and type of chord and the ordering of notes will determine the inversion.

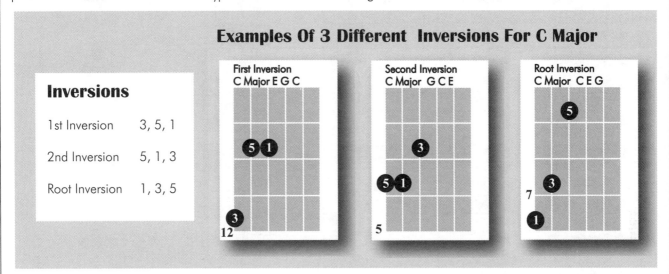

Examples Of 3 Different Inversions For C Major

Inversions

1st Inversion	3, 5, 1
2nd Inversion	5, 1, 3
Root Inversion	1, 3, 5

First Inversion C Major E G C

Second Inversion C Major G C E

Root Inversion C Major C E G

The Sound Of A Triad

The ordering of notes will change the sound of the chord. The change in the sound is quite subtle but it makes a big difference. Playing the notes in order (1, 3, 5) can get boring while leading with a note other than the note of the chord can introduce variety and contrast with other instruments. It is great to practice each inversion separately but mixing inversions based on the direction of the music and the location of the chords is more of a practical application. The first and second inversions will start with a note other than the tonic note of the chord. The root inversion will always lead with the tonic note of the chord. It is best to play the different inversions and hear the differences for yourself.

There is also a mechanical difference in the different inversions. The spacing of notes of the first and second inversion is usually closer than the root inversion. This closer spacing changes the feel of the chord as you play it. It also makes it easier. The root fingerings have a unique way of exercising your fingers. You may notice the first and fourth fingers are always holding down a note while the second and third fingers switch. The full examples are presented in a few pages.

Musical Spelling Of The Inversions

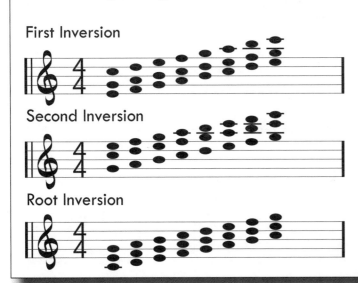

First Inversion

Second Inversion

Root Inversion

You can see the difference even if you do not read music! This is how you notate the chords of the different inversions.

The First Inversion. The degrees are 3, 5, 1. The notes for the C chord are E, G and C.

The Second Inversion. The degrees are 5, 1 and 3. The notes for the C chord are G, C and E.

The Root Position. The degrees are 1, 3 and 5. The notes for the C chord are C, E and G.

Notice the difference between the musical spelling of inversions on a staff. It will help you to remember them when you see them in written music.

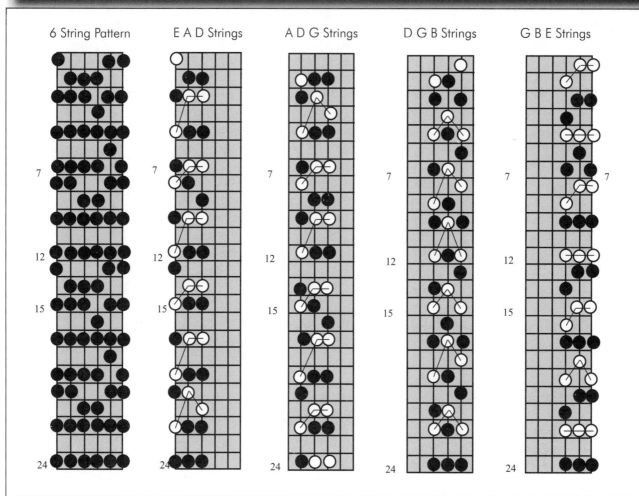

6 String Pattern — E A D Strings — A D G Strings — D G B Strings — G B E Strings

Identifying Three Note Triads

Triads like other chords will cascade down and across the fretboard. These are examples of chords cascading in the key of C major. In order to identify the triads in the diatonic pattern, it is helpful to break the six string pattern into three string sets. Notice each three string set is a smaller part of the diatonic pattern for C major. We break this out this way because triads contain three notes, one note per string. Using three string sets can make it easier to see the triads in the pattern. They are very easy to use this way.

The first fretboard contains the entire diatonic pattern for all six strings for 24 frets. The notes in each key are black. This is the diatonic pattern positioned for the key of C major.

The second fretboard contains only the lowest three strings. They are the low E string, the A string and the D string. Without naming any chords, do you see them cascading down the pattern? Do you also see that every note is used in building chords progressively? If you travel 12 frets using any three strings, you will play triads the seven basic triads for any key, and use all the notes in the process.

The third fretboard contains only the A string, the D string and the G string. Again, the triads are illuminated by the sets of white and black dots.

The fourth fretboard shows the D string, the G string and the B string. Notice that the pattern of triads repeats every 12 frets just like everything else does.

The fifth fretboard will show the highest three strings, the G, B and high E strings. These triads can be very fun to play. Many songs use them to climb through a key. They are excellent to use in a lead sequence.

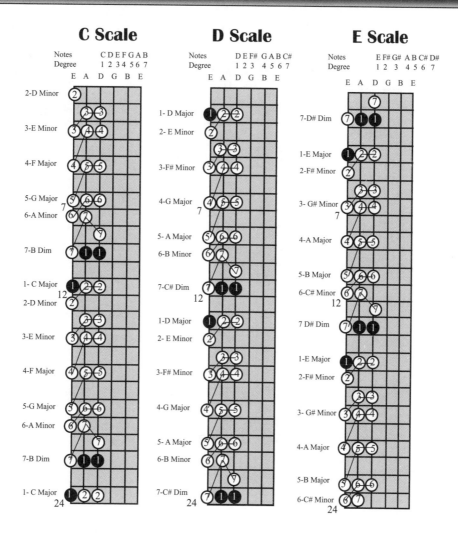

Naming The Triads

These three examples show you the same sets of cascading triads in three different keys. Notice when you move the pattern from the key of C major to the key of D major, the chords become the chords in the key of D major and get new names but maintain the same degree and the same form. What is a second-degree chord in the key of C major is still a second-degree chord in the key of D major. And it has only been moved two frets.

The first fretboard shows first inversion triads for the key of C major. The black notes are a quick guide to the tonic triad (C major). All the chords in the key of C major are present, and they repeat every 12 frets.

The next pattern shows first inversion triads for the key of D major. It is the same pattern as C major, but now it is moved up two frets. Notice that the tonic notes (black notes) are two frets higher than in C major. Also notice that the other triads are consistent between fretboards, but the names of the chords change.

Just to make sure that you understand this concept, notice that the third fretboard contains the very same information as the two previous fretboards but now it is two frets higher and in the key of E major. The relationships between the degrees of the key are maintained. The diatonic pattern automatically adjusts for major, minor and diminished chords as it is moved.

E A D Strings	A D G Strings	D G B Strings	G B E Strings	6 String Pattern

The First Inversion Triads

These are the first inversion triads for the key of C Major. Pay particular attention to the six-string pattern because it will not change for all three examples. In each example, the pattern is the same but the combination of notes will be different. By highlighting the notes of each inversion (ie. 1, 3, 5 or 3, 5, 1 or 5, 1, 3), the cascading chords are easily located. The different inversions can be in close proximity to each other. Look at the example below.

These are examples of C major. Notice that they are all in the same general area of the fretboard. They use the same notes too. In a very small geographical area, there are several chord choices available. This can allow for great expression without leaving a specific area of the fretboard. By choosing notes close to one another but different in character, unique and interesting harmonies can occur.

This example shows that you can play most chords in the same four fret area. This will hold true for all parts of the fretboard. When designing a song, it can be helpful to hammer out the chord progression using single inversion triads, but experiment using different inversions for the final product. Specific ordering of the notes can accommodate walking bass lines or contrary lines of motion or other effects.

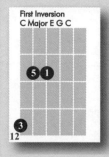

First Inversion
C Major E G C

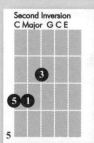

Second Inversion
C Major G C E

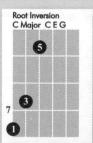

Root Inversion
C Major C E G

Second Inversion Triads

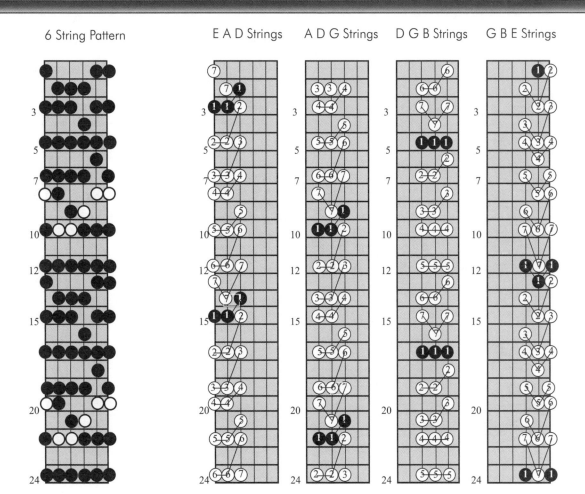

6 String Pattern   E A D Strings   A D G Strings   D G B Strings   G B E Strings

The Triads Of The Second Inversion

These are the second inversion triads. Notice they are positioned for the key of C major too. If you need a point of reference, look at the white notes or go back to the 12 Diatonic keys (pages 22-23). You should see that the pattern is exactly the same as shown for the key of C major. It is the very same pattern that is used for the first inversion triads. This time we have structured the relationships around the rules for the second inversion. The triads start with the fifth degree as the lowest. The second note is the first degree, and the last note is the third degree. For every 12 frets and every three string sets of strings, there are 21 chords (three inversions, seven triads per octave). At first this can be intimidating, but remember that once you learn the chords in the pattern, the information is easily transferred to other keys.

If you follow any three strings up the fretboard, you will notice that the degree increases for every new note. There is an orderly progression of notes used in the construction of triads. This is why triads cascade up and down the fretboard. In fact, every note is used in the construction of triads. Within the pattern is the complete information code for all diatonic keys.

Each inversion of triads has its own way of stacking chords which is determined by the ordering of the notes for the inversion. If you look back at the first inversion triads you can see the chord fingerings are different. But also notice that in each cascade, the major chords all use the same form and the minor chords all use the same form. The diminished triad uses a form that no other chord uses. The different forms the three inversions use will provide a separate personality for each set. The differences will show up in the sound of the triads. The only way to tell is to play each inversion and compare them. You must give your ear a chance to understand the differences by continuous exposure to the differences. Practicing this will definitely help your ability to distinguish between chords and inversions.

Root Inversion Triads

E A D Strings   A D G Strings   D G B Strings   G B E Strings   6 String Pattern

The Root Position Triads

One reason the root position triads are useful is because they are constructed with the root as the lowest note. If you are accustomed to playing single note scales, these are the triads most easily constructed for each note. If you follow a scale up and across the fretboard, you will play the root notes of these triads. If you want to construct a triad for any note, just add every other note (three notes) of the scale starting with the first note you are playing.

Notice that the lines connecting the triads proceed by spanning three to four frets for each triad. Triads that span four frets can be harder to play without muting or buzzing a note because it is harder to place fingertips correctly without touching other strings. When you play four fret triads, notice your index finger and pinky are always pressing notes and your second and third fingers alternate depending on the position of the third degree. This will limit the stretch needed to span the triads and give you an easy way to climb the octave.

The Scale Of C Major

Here is a scale of C major. The G note is the fifth degree of the C major scale and will spawn a G major chord. Go to the example above for the lowest three strings and notice there is a G major chord using a G on the E string (15th fret), a B on the A string (14th fret, shown in gray) and a D note (12th fret). Start by playing triads using the G major (5) triad and continuing up the scale just like the C major scale shown here. You should see the direct relationship between this scale and these triads.

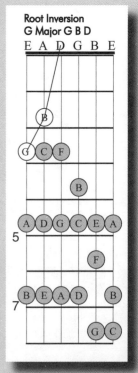

Root Inversion
G Major G B D
E A D G B E

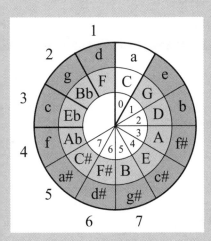

The Keys Of C Major And A Minor

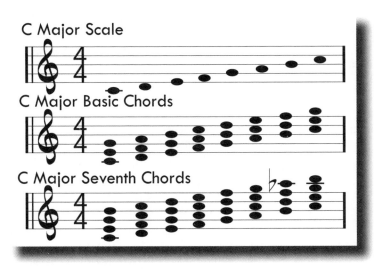

C Major Scale

C Major Basic Chords

C Major Seventh Chords

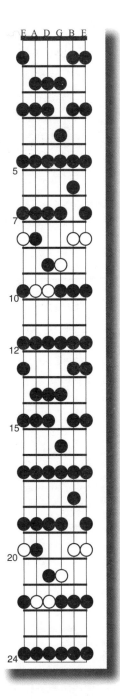

I	II	III	IV	V	VI	VII
Tonic	**Super Tonic**	**Mediant**	**Subdominant**	**Dominant**	**Submediant**	**Leading Tone**
C Major	D Minor	E Minor	F Major	G Major	A Minor	B Dim

IM7	IIm7	IIIm7	IVM7	V7	VIm7	VII7
C Maj 7	D Min 7	E Min 7	F Maj 7	G 7	A Min 7	B Dim 7

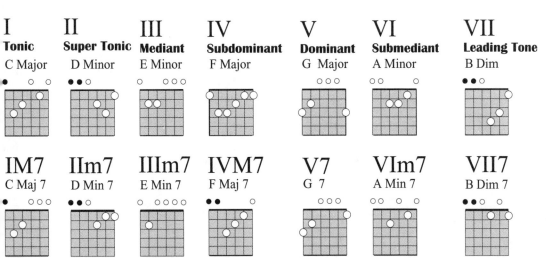

The Key of C Major

The next eight pages will cover the keys of C major and A minor. You will find the common basic and seventh chords in each key on the following pages. You will also find three inversions of the basic triads for the keys. The triads will serve as the fretboard map of the key for C major and A minor. The complete scale of C major and A minor is also present on page 38. The second half of the book contains twelve sections which will examine the keys for each stop on the circle of fifths, fully explaining each key.

The Circle of Fifths

Of all the concepts relating to music, the circle of fifths is the subject that is most often misunderstood. The Circle of Fifths is a major tool for understanding how all the different keys are structured and how they relate to each other. It is a tool that will allow you to look at music as a whole, not just disjointed parts.

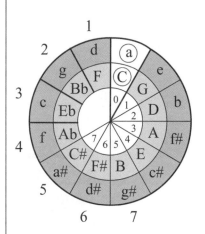

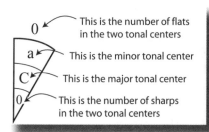

Let me also say this. This is not hard to understand. There are only a few concepts attached to the circle, so this is actually quite simple. Often times people try to look too hard into the circle and these simple concepts are overlooked. In this example we will look at the key of C major and A minor to see how these keys fit in the design of diatonic keys.

See how the slice taken from the circle contains spots for these two keys. **The letter 'a' is the minor key, A minor. The letter 'C' represents the major key, C major.** Both of these keys, A minor and C major share the same scale.

The notes in the scale are C, D, E, F, G, A and B. No sharps are present in this scale. **Notice the number '0' in the slice. This is the number of sharps in the key.** The key of C major and A minor do not have any sharps. No flats in the key translates to '0' in the slice. That is all the information this diagram expresses! The numbers on the outside of the circle tell you how many flats are in the key. Every key can be expressed in terms of flats as well as in sharps.

The chart of sharps and flats has been repeated on the next page so you can compare it to the circle and understand how they both describe the twelve major and twelve minor keys.

Moving Away From Tonic

How far can you move away from tonic? Think about this for a minute.

What is the farthest you can go before you start to approach it again. Look at the diagram below, it

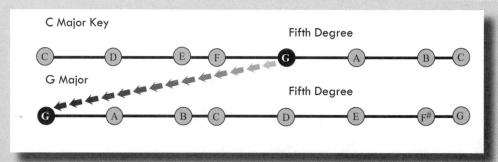

illustrates the different options for moving away from tonic. The fourth and fifth degrees represent the farthest distances you can travel from tonic before you start to approach it again. That is one of the concepts illustrated with the diagram on the next page. Notice the G and the F notes are the farthest away from the tonic note, C. Also notice that the fourth and fifth can be approached from both a forward and backwards direction.

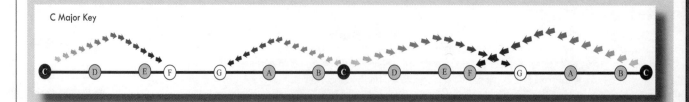

The Tonic Note Acts Like A Gravitational Force

All notes resolve back to tonic. All of the diatonic keys will be set up so that chords carved out of the key will naturally resolve back to the keynote. No matter what key you are working in, all the chords in the key will resolve back to the keynote and the chord of the keynote. The need to resolve is like the tug of gravity. It pulls the progressions towards the keynote and when it arrives at the keynote, it creates a feeling of rest. The piece has resolved and the resolution creates a strong desire to stay there. In this diagram C major serves as the keynote and everything revolves around it.

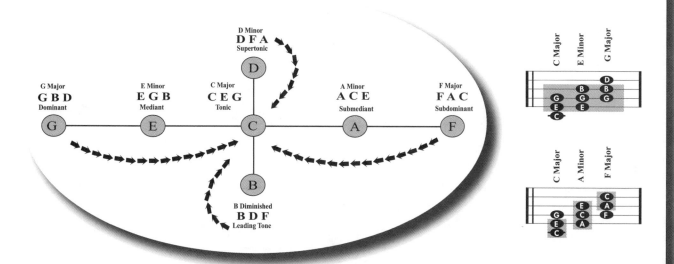

Substituting Notes And Chords

Notice that the E minor is half way between the tonic and the dominant chord. Also notice that the E minor shares two notes with both chords. The E minor shares the E and the G notes with C major and the G and B notes with G major. This means that the E minor can serve as a transition chord between the G and C chords. Or you can use this chord as an avenue to travel as you move back and forth between the G and C chords. The same type of relationship exists between the A minor chord and the C major and F major chords. The fourth and fifth chords represent the farthest points of travel within a key and the third and sixth degrees serve as midway points along these paths.

The Relative Minor Serves As A Hidden Door

The sixth degree also functions as a minor tonal center. All of these notes will resolve to the sixth note as well as to the major keynote. In addition, the minor tonal center can be modified to produce two new tonal centers, the melodic and harmonic tonal centers. So in effect, it acts like a secret door to more creative avenues. We will explore this in other keys as we go.

Chart Of Sharps And Flats For All Diatonic Keys

Key	Relative Minor	Sharps	Flats
C Major	A Minor	None	None
G Major	E Minor	F#	Bbb, Ebb, Abb, Dbb, Gb, Cb, Fb
D Major	B Minor	F#, C#	Bbb, Ebb, Abb, Db, Gb, Cb, Fb
A Major	F# Minor	F#, C#, G#	Bbb, Ebb, Ab, Db, Gb, Cb, Fb
E Major	C# Minor	F#, C#, G#, D#	Bbb, Eb, Ab, Db, Gb, Cb, Fb
B Major	G# Minor	F#, C#, G#, D#, A#	Bb, Eb, Ab, Db, Gb, Cb, Fb
F # Major	D# Minor	F#, C#, G#, D#, A#, E#	Bb, Eb, Ab, Db, Gb, Cb
C # Major	A# Minor	F#, C#, G#, D#, A#, E#, B#	Bb, Eb, Ab, Db, Gb
Ab Major	F Minor	F##, C#, G#, D#, A#, E#, B#	Bb, Eb, Ab, Db
Eb Major	C Minor	F##, C##, G#, D#, A#, E#, B#	Bb, Eb, Ab
Bb Major	G Minor	F##, C##, G##, D#, A#, E#, B#	Bb, Eb
F Major	D Minor	F##, C##, G##, D##, A#, E#, B#	Bb

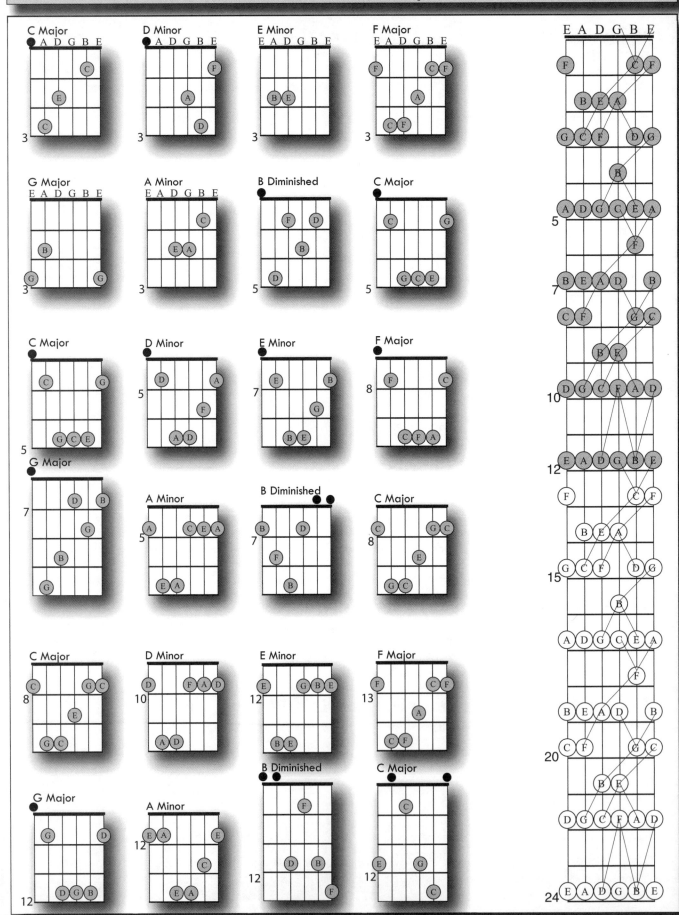

Seventh Chords

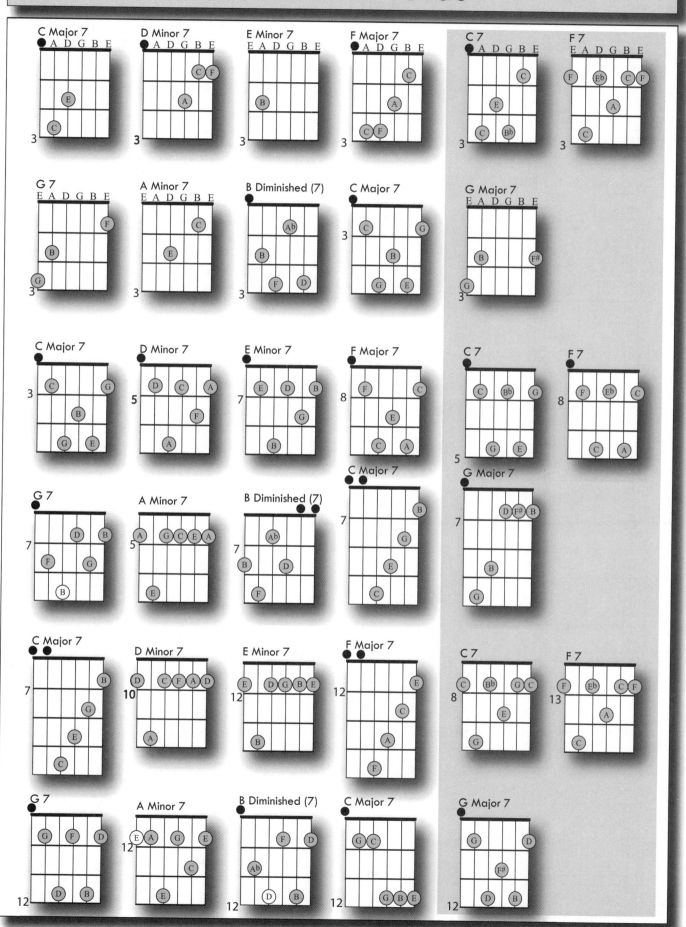

1st Inversion Triads For C Major

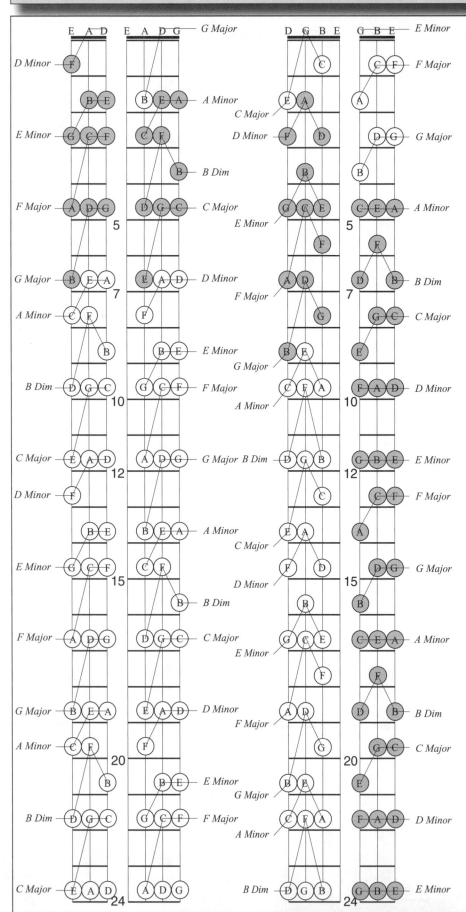

Three String Sets

The six strings of a guitar can be broken into four, three string sets. The lowest set contains the E, A and D strings. The two middle sets contains the A, D and G and the D, G and B sets. The upper set contains the G, B and E strings.

First Inversion Triads

The first inversion triads lead with the third degree of the chord. The first chord that can be formed on the neck of the guitar using the lowest three strings is D minor. These chords start by placing the third degree first.

Remember

D = 1st, F = 3rd and A = 5th for the chord of D minor.

The next chord is an E Minor. Notice the notes for E Minor are each one degree higher than for D Minor. Do you see that the tuning of the guitar makes progressive chord construction very efficient. By continuing up the same column seven chords, you will play every degree of the scale of C major once. Each set of strings contains one occurrence of each chord and then the column repeats.

You can also pick a path to the higher strings by following the gray dots. The gray dots point out just one route. They are included to provide a sense of movement across the neck as well as just climbing each column.

When you play each chord, do so by changing the different fingers used to form these chords. This will allow you to use any set of fingers necessary to play the chord. As a by-product, you will have greater finger dexterity. Notice that the fingerings for the first inversion are fairly easy to play. Each note is close to the others, so pressing the strings is easy. Pay attention to the sound of the notes played in the first inversion. They have a different sound than the second and root inversions. At first, concentrate on playing the progression of triads without making mistakes. Try to sound each triad cleanly. Staying in one column is easiest.

Second Inversion Triads

The second inversion triads lead with the fifth degree. Using the same notes as the first inversion triads, we can form second inversion triads.

Remember to play each note as cleanly as possible. Concentrate on making each note sound without buzzing. You should hear all three notes clearly.

Finger Picking

If you are trying to learn to finger pick, these triads can allow you to work both hands. Start out by plucking all three strings at once. This will allow you to keep the picking hand simple so you can concentrate on hitting the right notes cleanly. As you get comfortable, expand your picking patterns to increase variety and to test your understanding of the mechanics.

Once we have started constructing chords we simply climb the strings one note at a time. Because of the tuning of the strings, the different degrees of each chord are very close to one another and they climb the strings together.

The uses of these chords are varied and extensive. They are very useful for creating secondary parts for songs by applying different voicings to the main progression of chords. They also make excellent landing sites when mixing scale fragments with chords or arpeggios.

Triads built using the highest three strings can be quite playful. You can build a lead on top of them. Some of these are common chord forms such as the form used by the G major on this page. Do you see that if you play a C major open string chord (on the highest set), and slide it up to the 7th and 8th frets you would arrive at this G major chord? Move it two frets back and it is an F major. That is the one, four and five degrees, and they all use the same form.

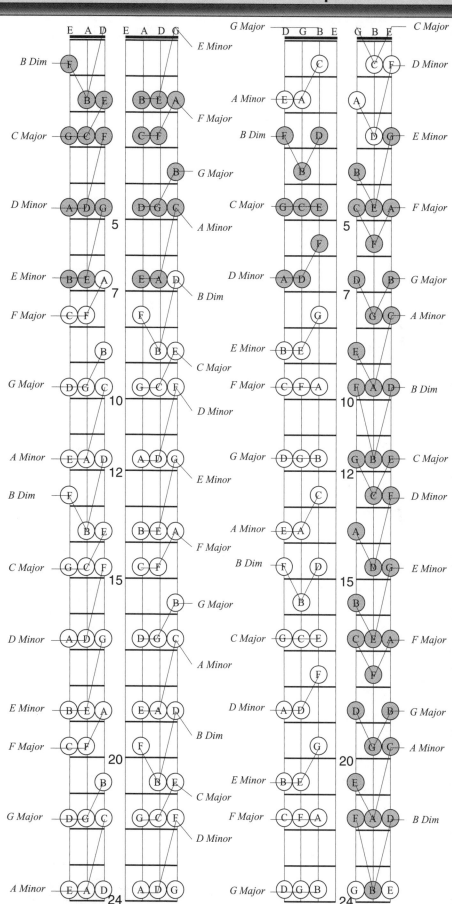

Root Inversion Triads For C Major

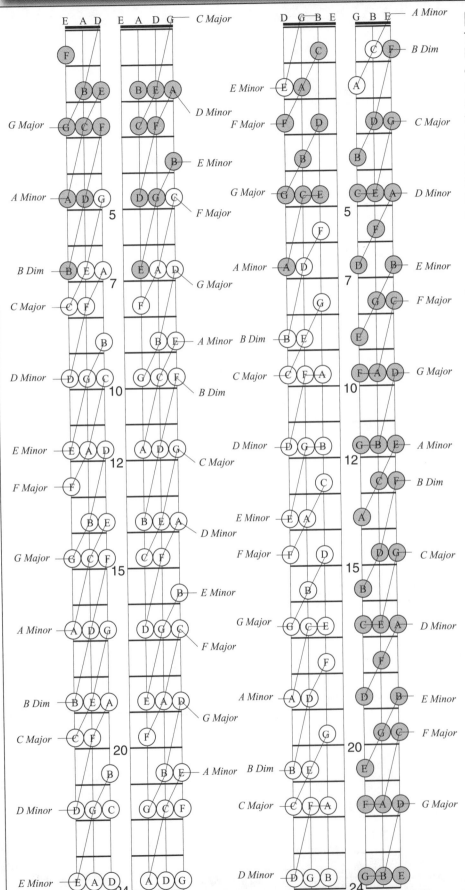

Root - Position Triads

The root position triads are constructed by stacking the first, third and fifth degrees of the chord in that order. The root position is easy to relate to the scale because the triad is based on the tonic note. Notice that the gray triads are based on the notes of the scale for the first four strings. Because the root position is based on the first degree, the third degree and then the fifth degree, it is easier to visualize chord construction using the root inversion.

Have you noticed that the root inversion has a different sound than the other two inversions? Did you also notice that the fingerings are different for the root position? These fingerings are farther apart in many instances.

As you climb through each scale, notice the particular sound of each degree of the scale. This will allow you to understand the sound of each position in the key.

The Gray Dots

Remember the gray dots provide a path through the scale for multiple octaves. If you play the triads that have gray notes, you will play the scale of chords in ascending order. As you look over the different paths available remember these are all options for travel and experimentation.

A Minor - The Relative Minor

A minor is one of my favorite keys. It is a very pretty key and lends itself well to acoustic ballads and love songs. It uses the same chords as C major, but it has a slightly different sound. It is excellent for ballads using an acoustic guitar. "Stairway To Heaven" by Led Zeppelin is an example of a song in A minor. If you know the song, look for the chords, they are right here.

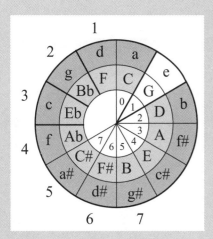

The Keys Of G Major And E Minor

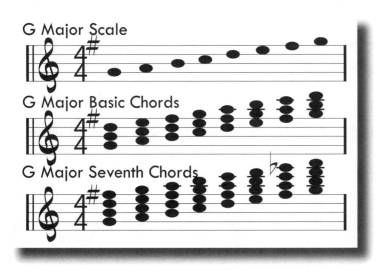

G Major Scale

G Major Basic Chords

G Major Seventh Chords

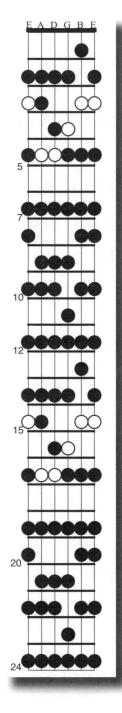

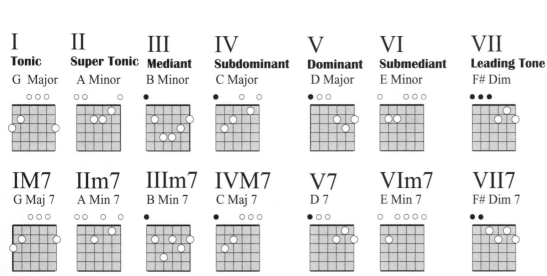

I	II	III	IV	V	VI	VII
Tonic	**Super Tonic**	**Mediant**	**Subdominant**	**Dominant**	**Submediant**	**Leading Tone**
G Major	A Minor	B Minor	C Major	D Major	E Minor	F# Dim

IM7	IIm7	IIIm7	IVM7	V7	VIm7	VII7
G Maj 7	A Min 7	B Min 7	C Maj 7	D 7	E Min 7	F# Dim 7

The Key of G Major

Look at the progression of seventh chords. These are the chords in the key of G major. These seventh chords have been built using only the notes inside the key of G. If you stick to the notes of the scale of G major, you will build this exact set of seventh triads. The progression is major 7th, minor 7th, minor 7th, major 7th, dominant 7th, minor 7th, diminished 7th. The fifth degree is also called a 7th chord. The dominant 7th term can be used in place of the standard 7th naming.

G Major And E Minor

The first key we worked in was C Major. This key, G major is next and will be slightly altered by adding a sharp to the seventh note, the F#. Every time we start a new key, the seventh note in that key will receive a sharp. The scale will also retain the sharps of previous keys. That process will start right here and continue in every key we build. The diagram will show you both keys, and how each one was created. It will also show you the spacing of notes and how these keys adhere to the rules of this exact spacing.

We are showing the key of F major too, because right on the other side of C major is F major. You can move forward or backwards from any point. Each key will repeat the same construction characteristics. Notice the spacing of notes is always the same.

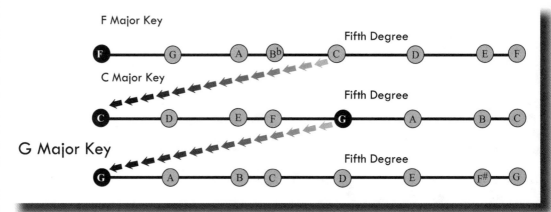

Note Spacing

We have discussed how keys are set up so all the notes provide a sense of revolving around tonic and supporting the key center. But we have not examined why this relationship is set up. The reason this happens when these notes are all together is because they adhere to the correct spacing of notes. If you use the notes that fall within this exact spacing, then the relationships will act the same way every time. That is why the degrees act the same way from key to key.

This spacing will be maintained in every key. The progression is whole step, whole step, half step. whole step. whole step. whole step. half step, starting on the keynote.

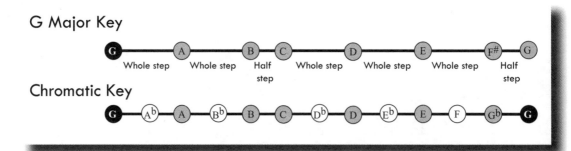

This exact sequence is what causes this group of notes to set up the key center and behave as a key. Once this exact spacing is present, the key will set up so that the notes behave like the diagram on the next page. The second line in the diagram above shows how the spacing is present with all notes. You just have to pick out the notes according to the spacing. This concept is at the very center of diatonic keys.

Incidentally, all the other types of keys, pentatonic, melodic minor and others will behave according to the rules of those specific keys because they have a unique spacing of notes that is carried through all the keys of that type. This is the basis of key centers.

How Chords Flow Through A Key

Take a good look at the chord progressions below. Notice all the chords flow alphabetically down the example towards the bottom of the page. The first example are triads. All of these triads are in the key of G major. The second set is based on the first example, only now full extensions are added to transform these mini-barre chords into full, six string barre chords.

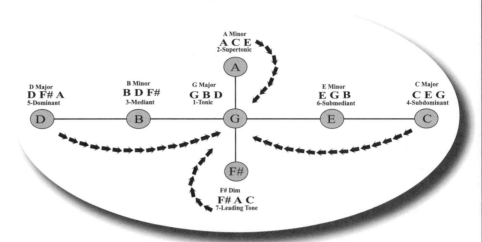

A Full Set Of Tools

Each one of these examples are powerful tools. How many resources do you have at your disposal? There are three primary inversions that occur in neat three string sets. There are also four, five and six string chords that borrow notes from the standard inversions. There are also some chord groups that do not occur on consecutive strings. There are also exotic variations of chords that will cover more than two octaves. These usually rely on a combination of open string notes and notes in the higher registers. So there are several cascades of chords you can use at any time. By combining chords from different inversions, a practiced guitarist has many opportunities to enhance a standard line of chords. These cascades of chords are an excellent way of understanding how keys work and they provide great exercises for your fingers.

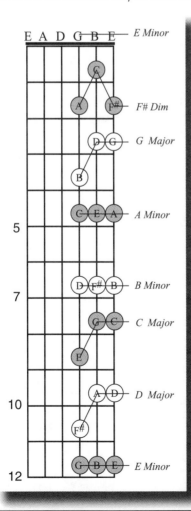

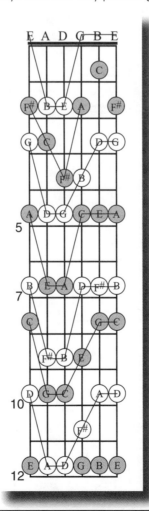

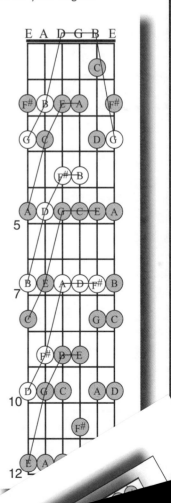

Basic Chords In G Major / E Minor

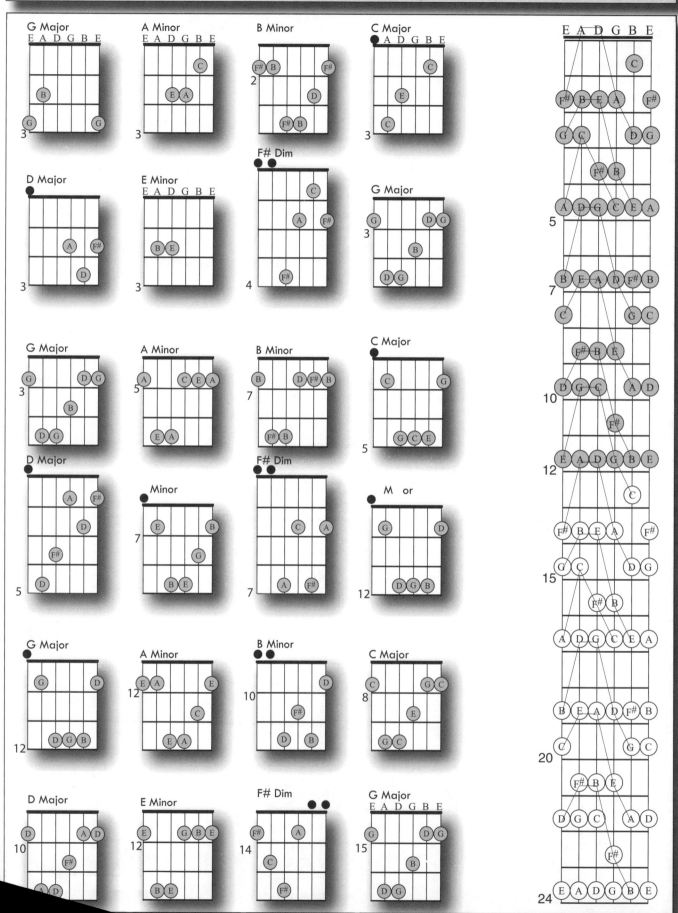

Seventh Chords

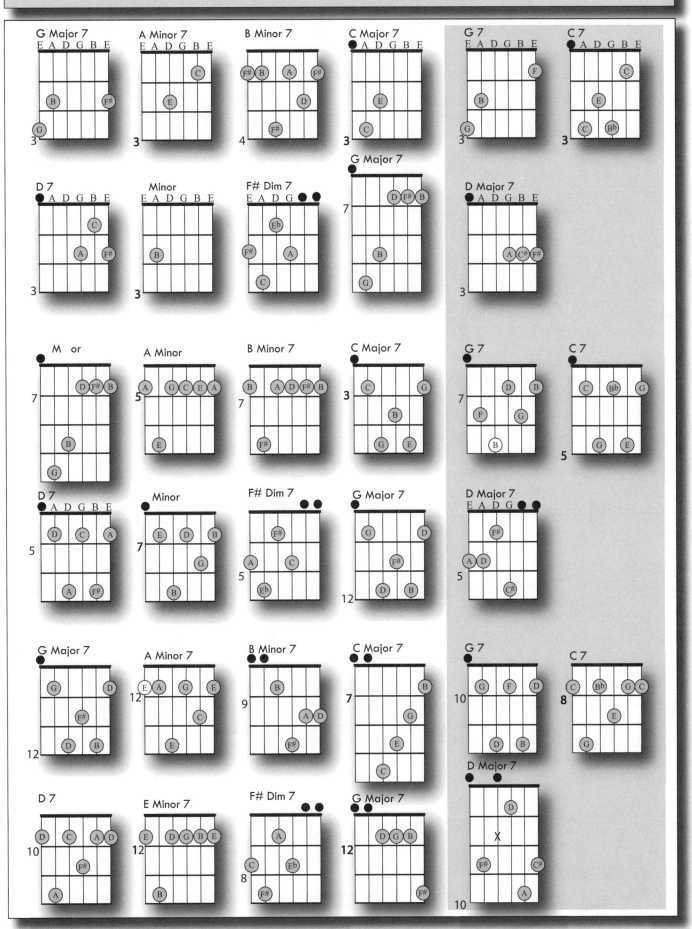

1st Inversion Triads For G Major

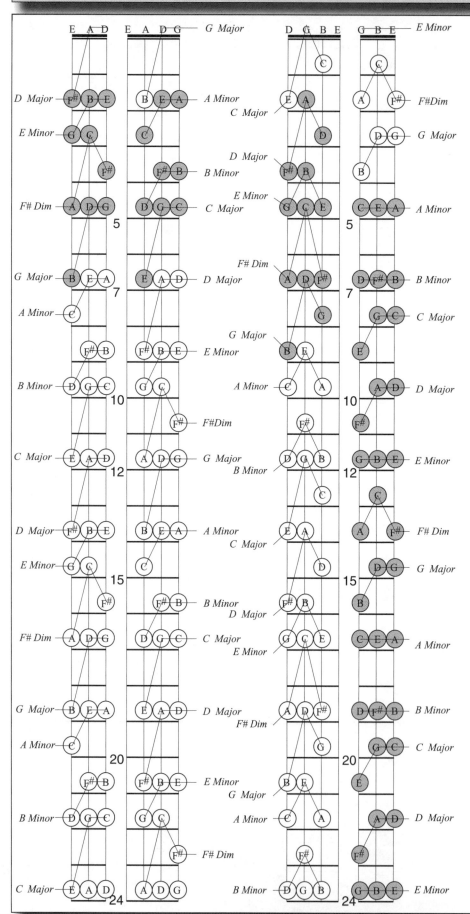

First Inversion Triads

The first inversion triads lead with the third degree and follow with the fifth, then the first. This will never change throughout the construction of these chords.

Notice a few things as we play the triads. The gray dots are a suggested way to progress up the key. If you play them sequentially, you will always play them in alphabetical order. In other words, try to start with the D major, then the E minor, then the F# diminished, then the G major. Notice that you have played triads only on the lower three string set. At this point, you can switch to the A, D and G strings and continue to climb through the key. With these same three strings play the A minor, the B minor and the C major. Play the D major, the E minor and the G major on the D, G and B strings. The rest of the chords can be played by either climbing these same strings or transferring to the G, B and E string. You do not have to use the path suggested here. You are encouraged to play all the triads in each column so that you become familiar with each chord and the relationships between neighboring triads. Jumping from column to column will develop your abilities to switch strings and change things up.

Notice that each column of triads contains seven triads and a complete set of chords for one octave. In other words, the E, A and D string triads start with the D major chord and continues with the E minor, F# Dim, G major, A minor, B minor and C major. That is seven chords and one complete octave. Of course, there is a D minor above the C major chord and the progression continues for as long as there are strings present. Do you see the triads continue in order? The graphic shows two octaves so that you can see how the fretboard repeats every twelve frets.

Second Inversion Triads

The second inversion triads leads with the fifth degree, then the first and then the third degree.

The Third column starts with a G major chord and is interesting because you play only open strings.

Advanced Study

Did you notice that the difference between the keys of C and G is the addition of a sharp to the F note in the key of G? Did you notice that by sharping that note, you are changing three chords for the key of G? The D minor in the key of C (D, F and A) is now a D major (D, F# and A). By sharping the F, the lower third (D to F) is now a major third.

The F major in the key of C (F, A and C) is now a diminished triad. This happens by sharping the F and changing the lower triad to a minor third. Now the chord is composed of two minor triads and is thus a diminished triad. Also, the B diminished triad in the key of C is now a minor chord by sharping the F and changing the upper third in the chord to a major. You have changed the overall triad from a diminished triad to a minor triad.

This will happen in this exact same way for every new key. We will always sharp the seventh degree to form a new key. This will change the triads based on the third, the fifth and the seventh degrees.

We don't talk at this level too much but you should know this happens at every key change. Be aware and be able to think at this level, because it will help you explain many things as you go.

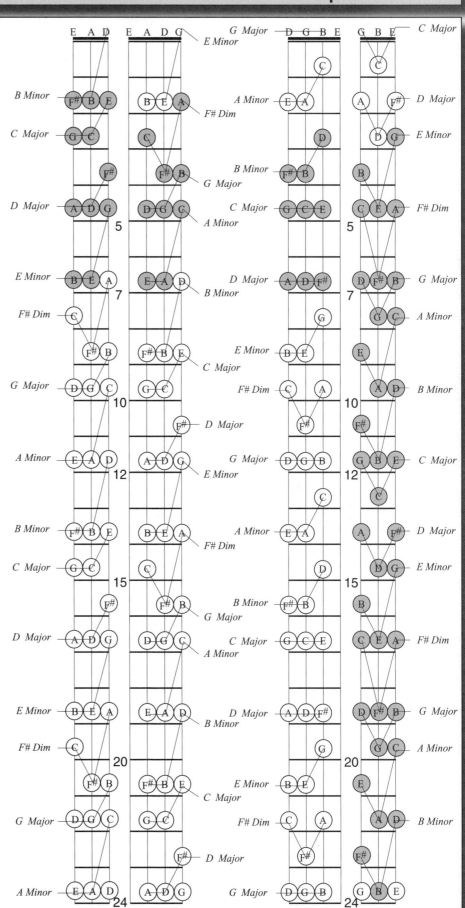

Root Inversion Triads For G Major

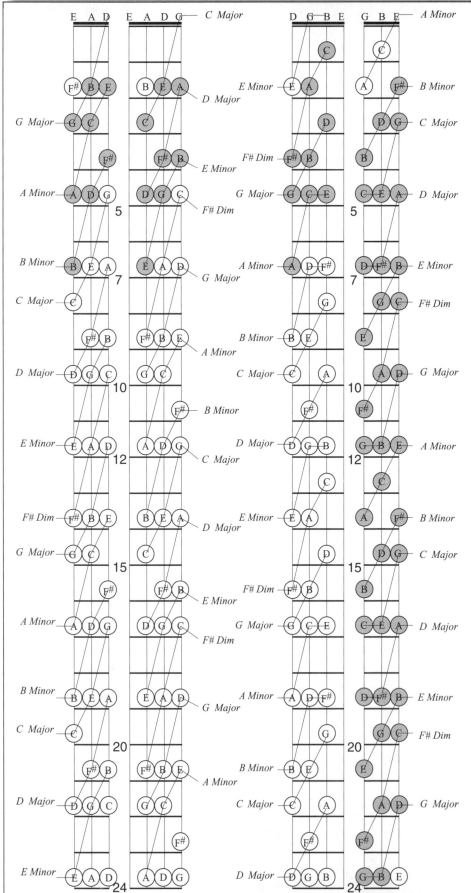

Root Position Triads

The root position triads are constructed by stacking the first, third and fifth degrees in that order. It is easy to relate the root position to the scale because the first note is the tonic note for the triad. Notice the root note of the gray triads are based on the first four strings.

It would seem that because of this relationship with the tonic note, the root position would be very valuable and it is. However the fingerings are somewhat awkward and the sound of the 1, 3 and 5 in this order are not necessarily the most pleasing. It is very predictable. It is important to recognize the different sound that is made by changing the inversion. The first and second inversions have two distinctly different sounds as does this position.

For most of my uses, I prefer the first inversion, both for the finger positions and the sound. In practical application it is common to see inversions mixed with little regard as to where a chord came from. However each inversion has a distinct quality and a value of its own. As for the ease of finger positions, the sound you are seeking should drive the use of the chord. It is also common to choose a chord because it can set up the next movement across, up or down the neck.

E Minor
The Relative Minor

Start on any set and play the E minor chord. Continue to play a scale of seven chords and notice that the chord of E minor brings the progression to rest.

Now do the same thing with the G chord and notice that the exact same chords will create the feel of the key of G. The G chord will bring the progression to rest. Both the G major chord and the E minor chord can serve as tonic. Each major key will have a minor key associated with it. This will greatly increase the possibilities for song creation.

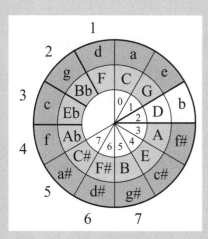

The Keys Of D Major And B Minor

D Major Scale

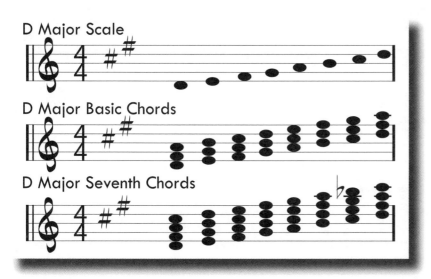

D Major Basic Chords

D Major Seventh Chords

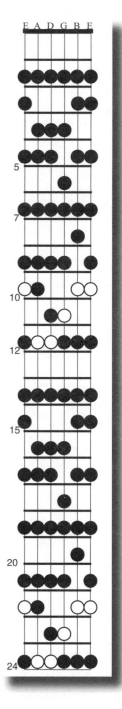

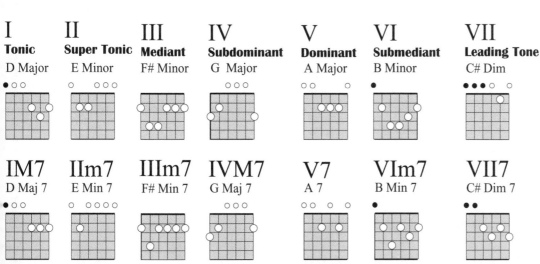

I	II	III	IV	V	VI	VII
Tonic	**Super Tonic**	**Mediant**	**Subdominant**	**Dominant**	**Submediant**	**Leading Tone**
D Major	E Minor	F# Minor	G Major	A Major	B Minor	C# Dim

IM7	IIm7	IIIm7	IVM7	V7	VIm7	VII7
D Maj 7	E Min 7	F# Min 7	G Maj 7	A 7	B Min 7	C# Dim 7

The Key of D

Notice that each basic chord can be altered to form a seventh chord. There are three different kinds of seventh chords used. The minor seventh, the major seventh and the dominant seventh chords. Just like the basic progression of chords in a key, the seventh chords will always behave this way inside the key. The chords on page 53, in the gray box all use notes outside the key. As you play them, see if you can hear the non key notes.

The Key Of D Major

The key of D major is built the same way the previous keys have been constructed.

Every time we build the new key, we go to the dominant chord (fifth degree) of the current key and construct the new key on that note. **We are using the dominant position as the gateway into the new key.**

This gateway concept can be exploited when designing chord passages. You can use

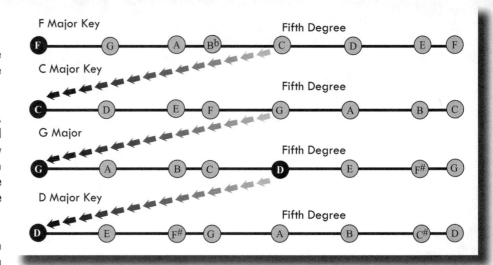

it to transition between keys or establish a new tonal center altogether. This is a powerful tool when you are stranded in a progression and need some force to break out. However learning to use the dominant position as a gateway will require some thoughtful training. One of the typical uses for this type of tool is to cycle through the circle of fifths as you play a standard progression and adapt it to every new key in either a forward or backwards cycle. You can always practice this as you work through each new key.

Why Do We Study The Circle Of Fifths?

Do you need to memorize this and be able to recite it on demand? The real answer is different for everyone. You may not need to have precise recall of this information. For some people, just acquiring an understanding of the basics is enough, (along with playing exercises using these chords). Other people will need a much deeper working knowledge of this tool. There are some serious reasons to explore this concept. For instance, the circle of fifths represents the whole world of diatonic keys. If you are trying to get your hands around the big picture, the circle represents the entire world of these standard keys. Knowing a little about this can you help develop your musical perspective. It can be a helpful tool for developing a mental picture of diatonic keys as well as what you like and dislike!

If you find yourself in a jam session and someone suggests moving the jam through the circle of keys, you have to be able to use the information on the spot. It is daunting to say the least, trying to figure out the next set of chords before it is time to play them. You do not need to try to memorize this all at once, cultivate your understanding over time. Let it slowly build over the course of the next few years.

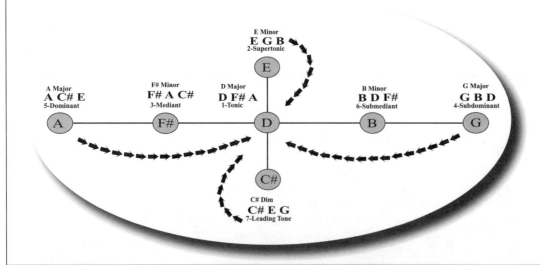

The Relative Minor

The minor keys are a very strong group. The minor connotation implies a lesser tonal center. Nothing could be farther from the truth. In fact the minor keys have three different variations which act as three different keys The minor grouping contains the harmonic, melodic and natural forms of the minor keys.

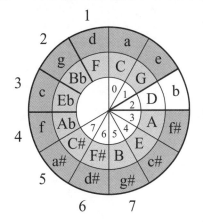

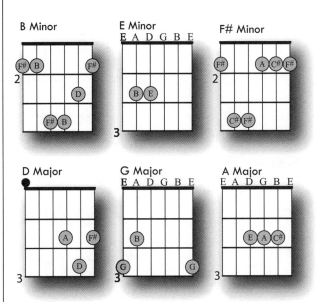

The Minor Group

Notice how the minor chords can set up just like the major chords do. They form the same relationships that are present in the major key. The major chords relate to the major scale as 1, 4 and 5 chords. The minor chords relate to the minor scale as 1, 4 and 5 chords. The two types of chords have quite different sounds. The minor chords have a lowered third note which creates the typical minor chord sound. So the minor tonal center will accentuate the minor sound. This means that these chord will set up to support either the major or minor center. They can be used in either one as well.

It may not seem obvious at first glance but these tonal centers are quite complex. A tonal center has very diverse uses and thousands of different sounds that can be crafted as the need arises. They are simple tonal centers but their uses are as numerous and diverse as your imagination.

The Harmonic Signature

Take a look at the major keys illustrated on the previous page. Notice that the seventh degree is always one half step behind tonic. This sets up a very special relationship between the seventh degree and tonic. Since the pull of tonic is very strong, the seventh degree leads right into tonic. Being so close to tonic accentuates the feeling of resolution when tonic is achieved.

But the minor key does not have this type of relationship. The seventh degree in the B minor key is A. A is a whole step away from B. In order for the minor key to have this same relationship, the harmonic form was introduced. The harmonic form adds a sharp to the seventh degree, which is the A note. Sharping the A note creates the same sense of tension available in the major key, because the A# is right next to the G note.

The harmonic key provides the minor group with the same structure that is present in the major key. So in a sense the minor key is more versatile than the single form of the major tonal center.

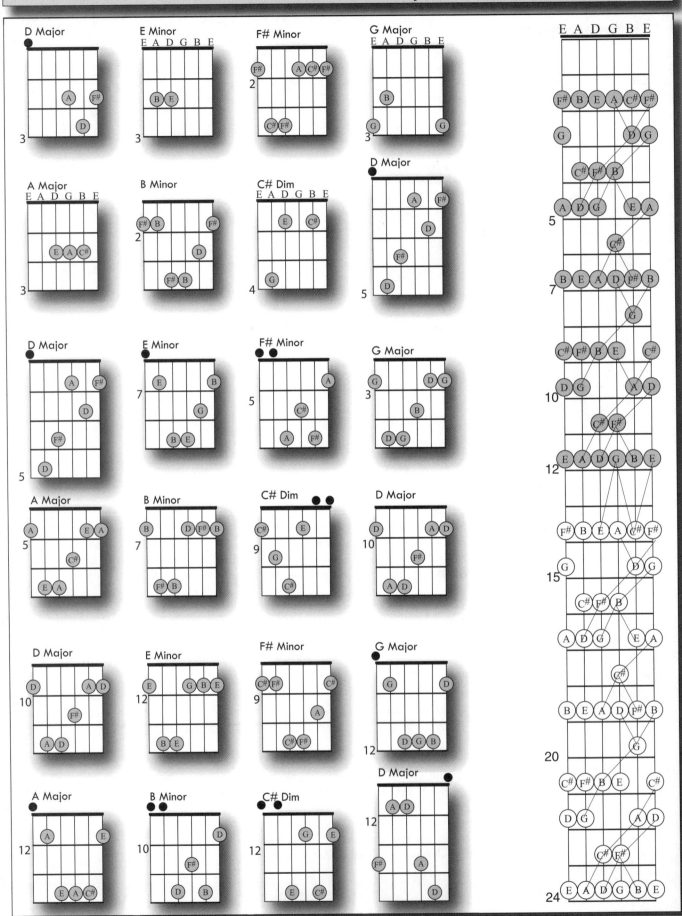

Seventh Chords

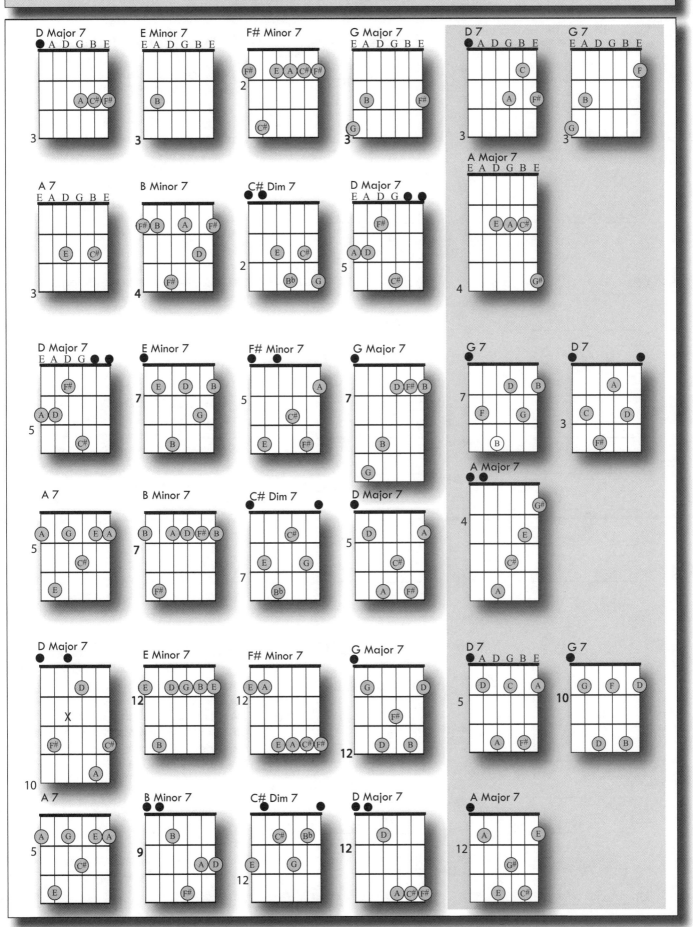

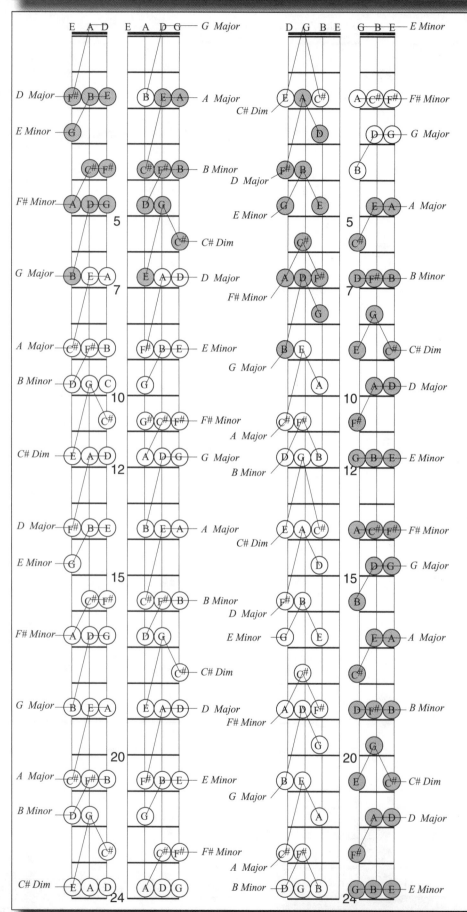

First Inversion Triads

The first available chord in the first inversion of this key is a D major. Notice that two open strings are used in the construction. Using the G, B and E strings, the first chord is played entirely with open strings. It is also important to realize that the next open string is D and you can play it with any triad played with the highest three strings. It will create a drone effect and emphasize the tonic note and the key.

Peeling off a lead line is also very easy using the scale of D major and mingling various triads based on the high three strings. Remember that if you do not like the voicing or the fingering of a particular chord, look at the various inversions. Chances are there is a suitable chord in a different inversion very close to any position.

Advanced Study

If you are confused about any part of chord and scale construction, identify what part that is. For me, it was the diminished chord. Then examine in detail the differences in the scale as we change keys. Track the differences as the scale changes. Use enharmonic spellings for various keys if you are having trouble examining a key using flats or sharps. If you are able to identify areas that give you trouble and then pay special attention to them, you can strengthen your weakest areas. This will almost always result in elevated abilities.

Start With Two Guitars

If you are thinking about playing lead lines over these chords, I suggest you recruit another guitarist to help you explore them. While one player holds down a rhythm line using a string of these chords, the other guitarist is experimenting playing over the chords with the scale of D major.

Look for areas of the scale that sound the best when played over the chords, and then create playful statements using these same areas. Try the open string scale and then move into the higher pathways. Some areas will sound better than others.

Second Inversion Triads

The second inversion triads lead with the fifth degree. Look at the D major chord using the highest strings. This is a major chord form. The distance between the lower third is two whole steps. If you want to change the form into a minor form, lower the third which changes the lower third from major to minor. Now look at the E minor just above it. This is the same form except the lower third is a minor third. In other words, the distance between E and G (the lower third) is a half step and a whole step. It is the change in the lower third that is responsible for altering the form.

If you are having trouble determining the distance between thirds, you can go to any string in the two octave scale diagram and examine the distance between the notes in question. It is a helpful way to get comfortable with distances and major and minor thirds.

Remember our discussion of the progression of chords through the scale as maj, min, min, maj, maj, min and diminished? Look at the D major chord again. Starting there, ascend up the neck. Notice that the pattern of maj, min, min, maj, maj, min and diminished is maintained. To see the C# diminished chord you have to look one step below the D Major chord (towards the nut). Do you see it? Do you see that the flow of chords is circular? Remember that a new set of identical chords is one register higher on these same strings.

There are many examples of repetition of the fretboard. Notice on the D, G and B strings the A Major chord is present, also the B Minor above it uses the A Minor open string form. This form is used for all minor chords on these strings.

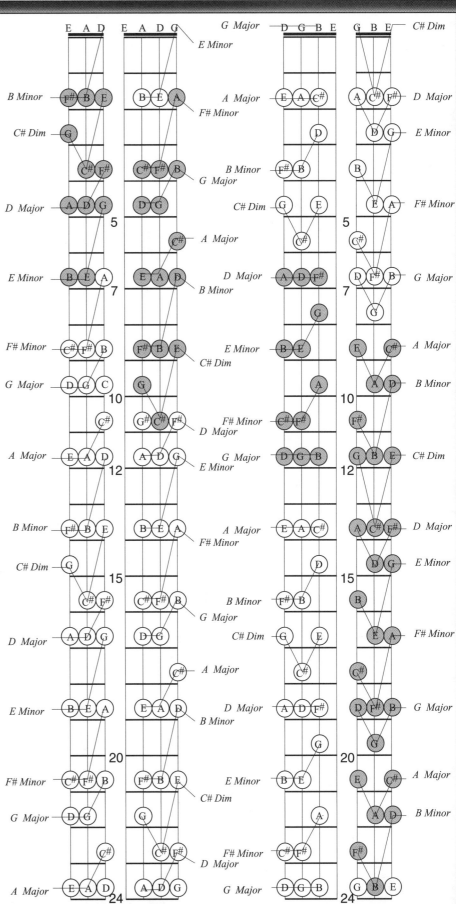

Root Inversion Triads For D Major

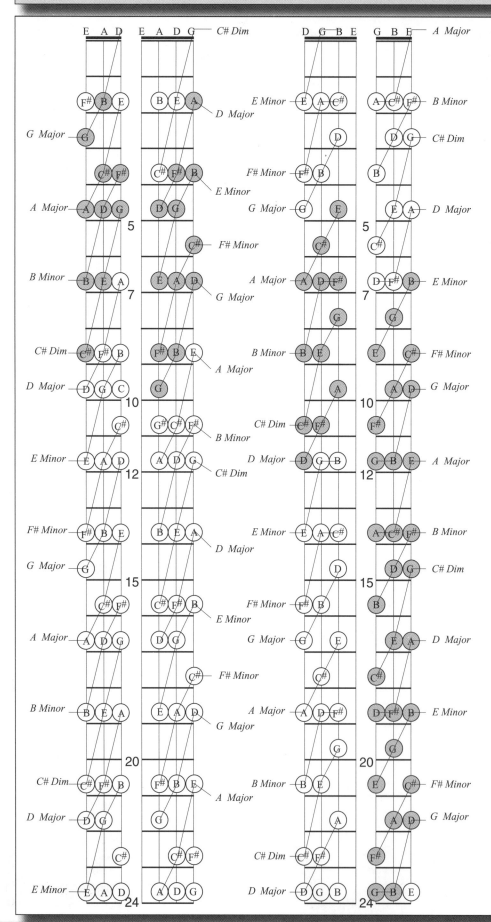

Root Position Triads

Here is the scale path that the root of each chord follows across the fretboard. Each one of these notes spawns a triad in this example alone.

Notice that the root notes only extend to the fourth string (shaded notes). Since the triads occupy three strings, the root position can only climb to the G string.

If you need the triads for the upper four strings, use the first inversion. Use the second inversion to work with tonic notes in the middle four strings.

The G major chord below shows an example of the chords that are spun from the root notes shown here in gray.

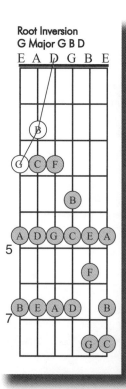

Root Inversion G Major G B D

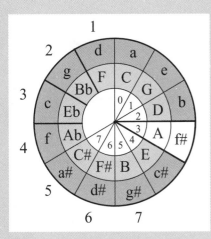

The Keys Of A Major And F# Minor

A Major Scale

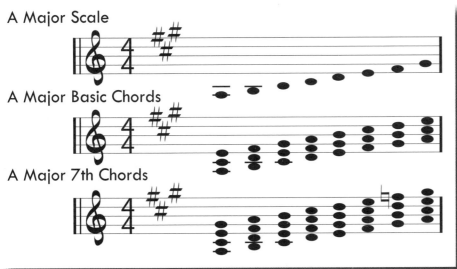

A Major Basic Chords

A Major 7th Chords

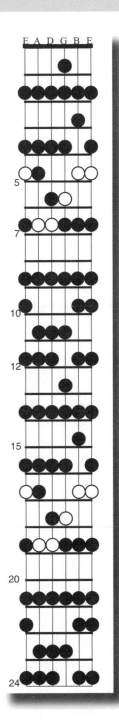

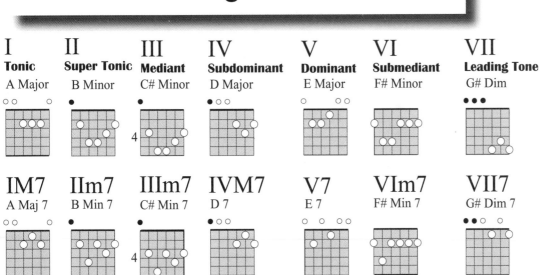

I	II	III	IV	V	VI	VII
Tonic	**Super Tonic**	**Mediant**	**Subdominant**	**Dominant**	**Submediant**	**Leading Tone**
A Major	B Minor	C# Minor	D Major	E Major	F# Minor	G# Dim

IM7	IIm7	IIIm7	IVM7	V7	VIm7	VII7
A Maj 7	B Min 7	C# Min 7	D 7	E 7	F# Min 7	G# Dim 7

The Leading Tone

Notice the leading tone is off by itself. Remember the leading tone is a diminished triad, two minor thirds stacked to produce an imperfect fifth. Consult the triad construction pages if necessary. The leading tone triad is very unstable. By itself it sounds awkward because the relationship between two minor triads creates a lot of tension inside the chord. When played in a progression the leading tone relates strongly to tonic and will intensify the feeling of rest once tonic is achieved.

The Meaning Of The Circle Is Simple

After constructing four keys, you can see that the information the circle communicates is simple. All it does is tell you the names of the major and minor keys, the number of sharps or flats and the position in relation to the other keys. The circle expresses the exact position of each key, relative to all twleve keys. That's it!

The circle is an opportunity to see all twelve major and all twelve minor keys in context with each other. It can serve as a reminder of what is present and what options are most obvious.

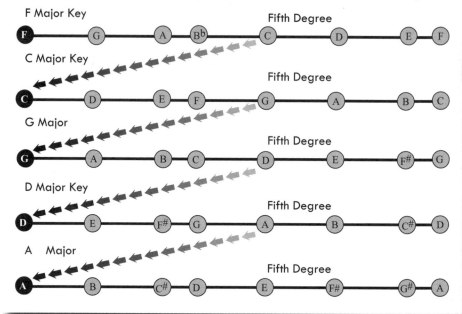

It can help you to remember what sharps are present and you may be able to cycle through the chords in a key. Once the construction techniques are understood and the ability to use the tool is developed, you may find the circle starts to help you sort out what you want and what you need to focus on. It is common to be more familiar with the first five or six keys and less with the last six. If you continue to examine the whole circle of keys, you may start to address the areas you know least well.

Gateways Inside A Tonal Center

Every key contains several gateways to different keys. Actually every degree in a scale points to another key. These are all gateways to new keys and new opportunities to change direction. You can use a progression in a key to transfer to another key by various means. So instead of just having seven notes at your disposal, the entire palette can easily be accessed and present opportunities to go wherever you want, using any of these portals. If you need more options, just transfer to a key that presents a direct opportunity to transfer to the key you are ultimately interested in.

You can cycle through to the next key, the relative minor key, or any other key that is represented by a note in this scale. The degree of success you achieve in moving from tonal center to tonal center will be determined by how thoughtful and creative your approach is. Every solution to this will be different and totally hand crafted.

The graphic above will help you to see the other keys in context to this one. You may want to turn to page 125 and see them all.

The relative minor tonal center also shares the same name as the key located three tonal centers ahead. Remember there is an F# major key and an F# minor key.

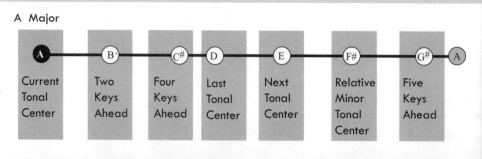

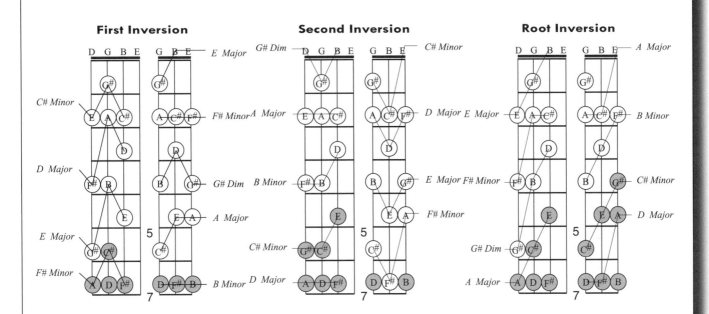

Working Horizontal As Well As Vertical

These are standard cascades which are shown on the following pages. It is very helpful to use them in a vertical fashion. Working vertically allows for wholesale movement up and down the fretboard. Triad cascades can facilitate moving up or down because you can see the paths for movement. However there is another component to consider.

You will also find a wide variety of chords in a very condensed manner for all areas of the fretboard. This is very important. There will be many instances where quick accent chords are helpful for disguising the basic melody or enhancing a plain progression.

These additional chords can be reached with very little added movement. All you have to do is take the time to notice what chords are right under your finger location and make the effort to play and combine them.

It can be difficult to see what a person is playing when these type of chords are injected. The movements are so small and precise and the alteration is usually significant enough to notice the difference in sound but not how it was accomplished. So it is hard to see exactly what was done to change or alter a progression.

Another benefit of convenience is they are readily available when playing a lead line. A well positioned chord inside a linear line of notes will fill out the sound. Your ear expects to hear a linear phrase but instead some chordal movement occurs with or inside the phrase, and the contrast to the single note line is noticeable and very often creative.

Interspersing chords with single note lines is the realm of advanced players. Not only do you need to understand these tools are available, you have to create the arrangement and set up the effect and be able to do the move. That is a major reason why these types of cascades should be incorporated into your playing, specifically with scales. These chords are actually three note scales, but when used in the context of a song they become electrifying tools that set up an emotional tug with the listener.

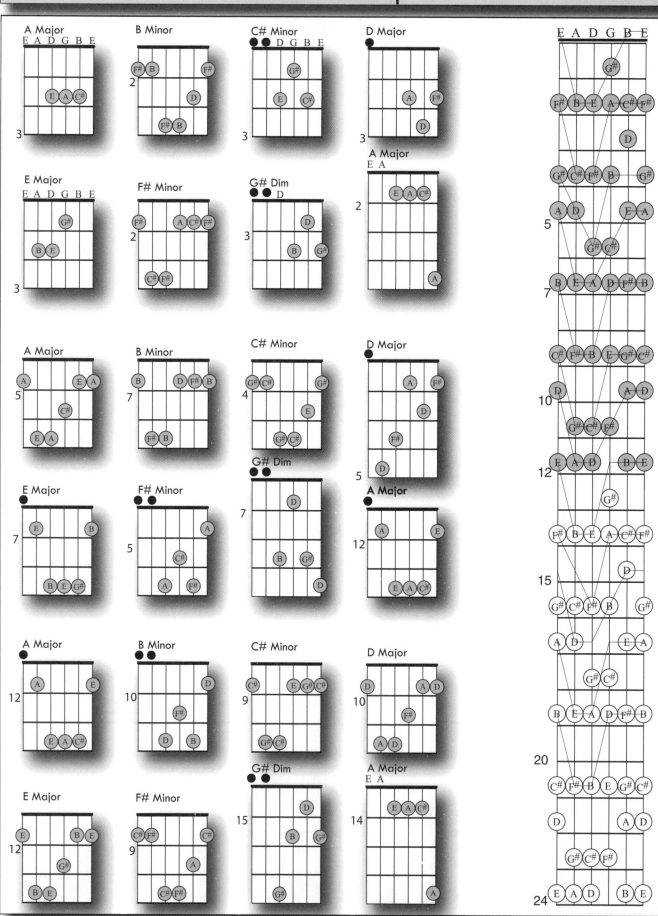

Seventh Chords

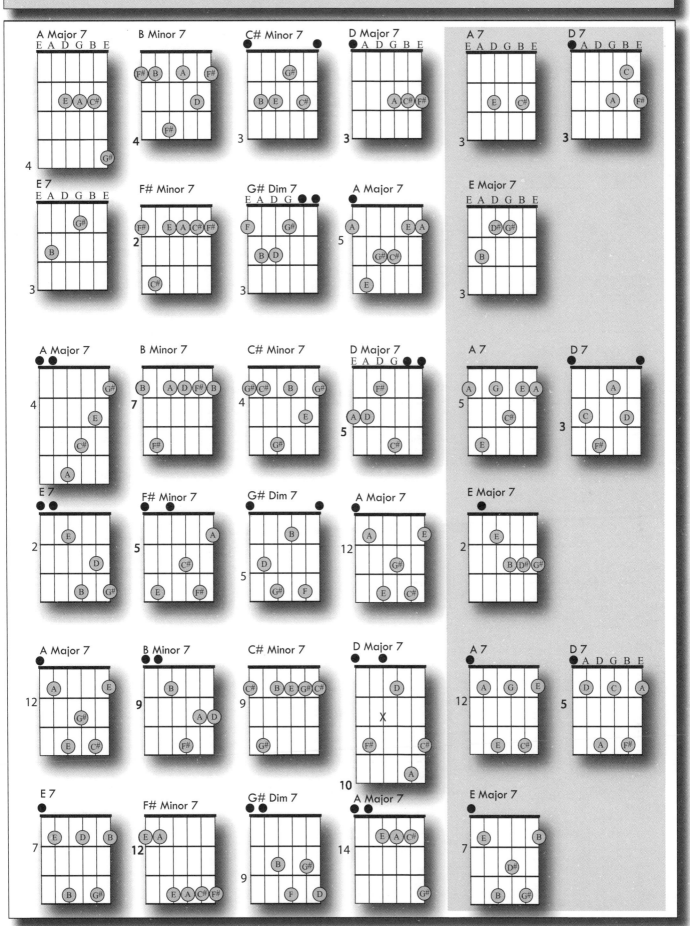

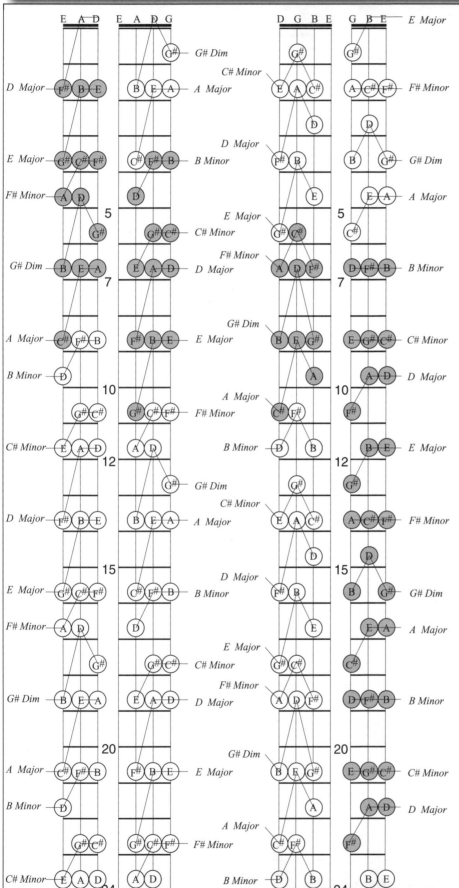

First Inversion Triads

First inversion triads are good for flat picking exercises. The spacing for the notes is very close across the strings and the challenge of flat picking the notes as you work the scale is excellent exercise for both hands as well as the combined coordination required to flat pick.

Play the scale on the same set of strings from top to bottom by strumming or playing the chords in your usual way. Get comfortable with the fingerings before you introduce something different. Now flat pick the same progression of chords, lowest note first, striking all three notes once before moving to the next chord. Stay on the same three strings.

Practice this slowly at first. You must go slow enough to strike each string and sound the note cleanly. Keep it simple. If you are having trouble doing this, try staying on one chord until you can pick all three notes cleanly several times in a row without making a mistake. Next move between two positions that have the same form so that you do not have to complicate the dynamics by adding an additional element. Gradually mix in other chords until all can be played.

This may require quiet time that allows you to tune everything else out and concentrate intently on this process. If you concentrate and work hard, you will get better almost every time you play. It may take a few times before your hands loosen up and perform correctly. This exercise will give you much more control of your flat picking.

After you can play up and down the set of strings, try switching strings as you climb through the scale. This will introduce a new dynamic and test to see if you can switch strings and still remember where to place your fingers and strike the strings.

Each time you introduce another component into this equation, you test your ability to do this correctly with the new addition. You will find some additions will cause you to make mistakes.

Second Inversion Triads

Examine different ways of looking at these chords. Notice that the A major chord using the D, G and B strings is directly across from the D major chord using the G, B and E strings. Remember that the 1st chord and the 4th and 5th chords have a very strong relationship. Also notice the E major right above the D major.

You do not always have to practice this material in a linear fashion. Identify the sounds you enjoy the most and apply them to different keys and different positions on the neck. Don't just recite this information, breathe life into it by experimenting with it.

As you play the A, D and G progression, practice playing it different ways. It is interesting to realize that you can play the three chords without ever lifting your ring finger. Playing the A major chord, play the C# with the ring finger. That puts it on the B string. Use that finger to play the D note in the D chord and the E note in the E major. Do not pick it up as you change chords. This can be applied to many other chords. It can be an effective way of creating a distinct sound.

Here is another example of this trick.

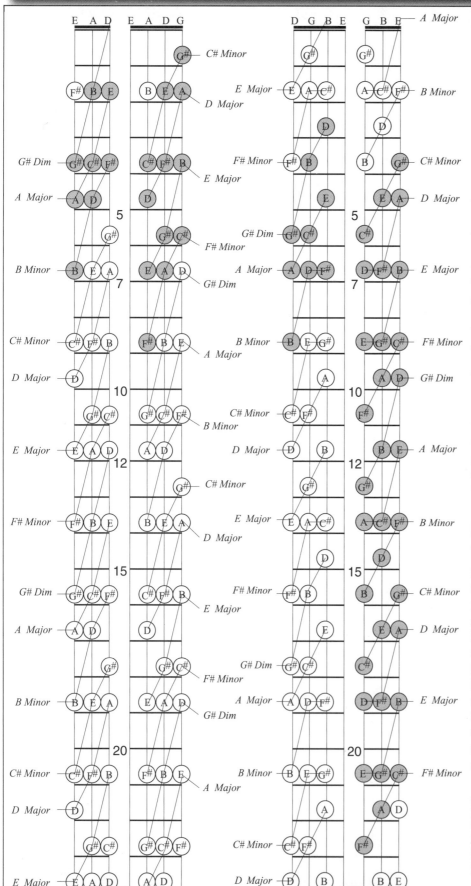

Root Position Triads

If you can flat pick with no problem using the first and second-inversion triads, try it with the root-position triads. If you are not accustomed to the stretch and the fingerings, you may have some trouble.

For me it is easiest to use my index and pinky fingers for the high and low notes and alternate using my ring finger and my second finger for the middle note. That way, my fingers are in position and will not become fatigued as easily because they are not constantly stretching. On the other hand if you are playing it that way and having no problem, try playing these triads with three consecutive fingers. It should test your stretching ability. The idea is to mix it up in an effort to know the information as well as possible. It will show up in your performance!

This kind of finger and hand strength will be very helpful when you are striving to play something new or hard. If you are improvising, this information will show up sooner or later and influence your personal style. You may be able to create sounds you were not able to before. Expect to use it in a creative way.

F# Minor
The Relative Minor

Remember to practice these chords in terms of the relative minor. If you do not remember to think of terms of the relative minor you might think you are in the major key when you are not. This can happen during an improv if you are not careful. It has happened to me more than once and it can be a problem if you are trying to end a song by moving towards what you think is tonic, only to find out you are trying to end a song in a minor key by using the related major note. This will not work and at first you may not know why!

Notice This

Notice on the A, D and G strings, the B minor occurs only once. This will also happen with the G# Dim chord on the G, B and E strings.

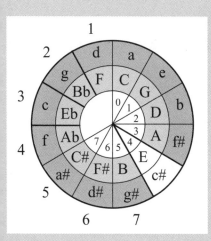

The Keys Of E Major And C# Minor

E Major Scale

E Major Basic Chords

E Major 7th Chords

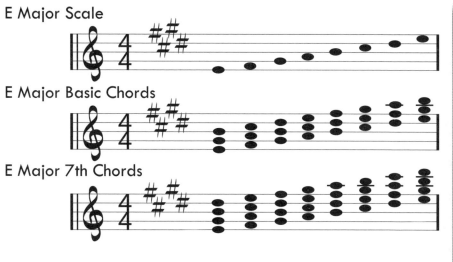

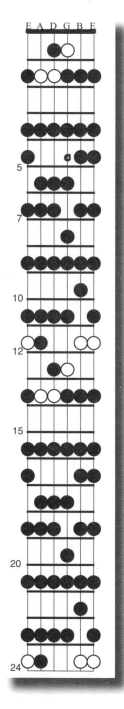

I	II	III	IV	V	VI	VII
Tonic	**Super Tonic**	**Mediant**	**Subdominant**	**Dominant**	**Submediant**	**Leading Tone**
E Major	F# Minor	G# Minor	A Major	B Major	C# Minor	D# Dim

IM7	IIm7	IIIm7	IVM7	V7	VIm7	VII7
E Maj 7	F# Min 7	G# Min 7	A Maj 7	B 7	C# Min 7	D# Dim 7

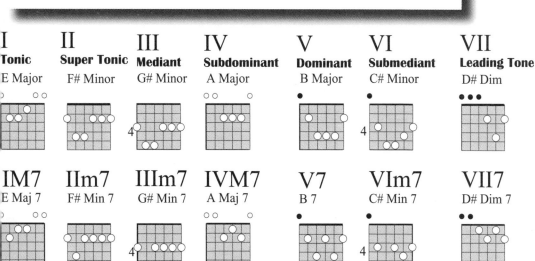

Typical Progressions

There are several typical progressions that have appeared in songs too numerous to list. One of the standards for rock and roll is the 1, 5 and 4. Playing the 1, 5, 4 (degrees) in the key of E is particularly common. Use the open E and the B note on the A string, hammer the C# on the A string from the B and then switch to an open A note and an E note on the D string, hammering the F#. This is playing fifths and hammering the sixth.

The Construction Of A Key

With five keys articulated we are almost half way around the circle.

This is a good time to look at the sharps being inserted and notice what they do.

Take a good look at the spacing of notes in this diagram. All of these notes must fall within the gray areas articulated. In order for that to happen, each scale must be modified so their notes fall within the correct area. Conveniently you can add sharps according to the formula and alter each one in a way that allows the scale to adhere to the rules and be unique within this group.

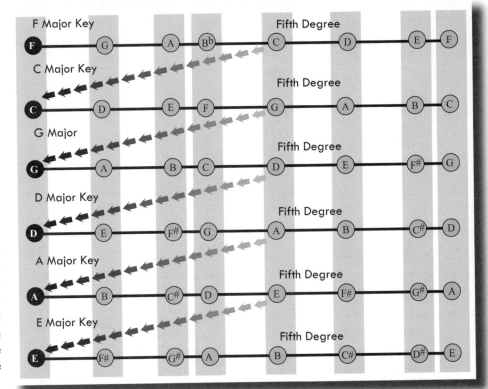

Adding Sharps To Create The Key

The key of E has added another sharp to the seventh degree in order to make the scale fit the rules. But the sharps that are carried over from the previous keys also allow for the scale to fit the whole step and half step criteria. So everything that has happened in these scale construction techniques is meant to further define the keys and arrange them in a way that allows for the relationships to form.

That means we are talking on a physical level as well as an auditory level. In other words, not only does this concept govern the physical location of notes, but it also causes the notes to revolve around a tonic note and set up a tonal center that is consistent with the other keys in the group. Remember it is the spacing of notes that allows for the diatonic sound to occur and for the tonal relationships to set up. This is facilitated by adding sharps to keys so they can conform to the rules. This is actually very complex theory and it boggles my mind that people hundreds of years ago came up with instruments that were designed to facilitate this theory and turn it into practical application. If you just play a few chords and never delve into the rules and the concepts, these complex relationships never become clear.

Ideas For Songs

When I write song passages, I often times have this book present and open. If I am working in the key of E, I will turn to the pages containing first and second inversion triads, and I will look at routes for the chords I have already chosen. I will also look for new chords to use and variations that happen to offer some tasteful voicing or move in the direction I am interested in.

The key of E major offers several different cascades that contain the majority of options for this key. Below are four different cascades for the key of E major. You can work to any area of the fretboard, you can switch to different chord types and you can isolate specific notes and transition to any of these other chords. All of these tools offer limitless choices for improvisation and song construction. If you incorporate these cascades into your song writing process, you will start to isolate areas that appeal to you and take advantage of the ease in which you can experiment and create. I find these tools will provide structure and add new options, if I just work out with some of these concepts.

Exercises

The exercises you can generate with this material are almost as limitless as the potential for song creation. Here are some basic suggestions.

1. Just play the progression of chords as they occur. Play the notes and make them sound clean.

2. Pick a simple pattern as you play each chord. Pick the passage repeatedly until you can switch chords and keep the picking steady. When you master this, do it some more!

3. Play the I-V-IV progression using every combination on this page. Make up your own passages and repeat them using different chords in the key of E major.

4. Find a few chords you like and concentrate on only those chords. Create a simple progression. Then pick a few more and repeat it. Play the scale of E major and then play any of the chords here while maintaining a slow rhythm. You are trying to explore linking slowly, so you have more time between moving your fingers.

5 Try these combinations, I-V, I-IV, I-III-VI-V-I. Also try playing the I-IV-II-V-I. Try the I-IV-I-V-VI-III-I and I-IV-I-V-VI-III-ITry playing the same progression using several different cascades. The same progression will sound different because of the different inversions or location of the chord on the fretboard.

6. Examine what you need help with and design chord exercises that workout your weak areas. The more time you spend exercising in these areas, the better your tactile response will become. **You can turn a weakness into a strength!**

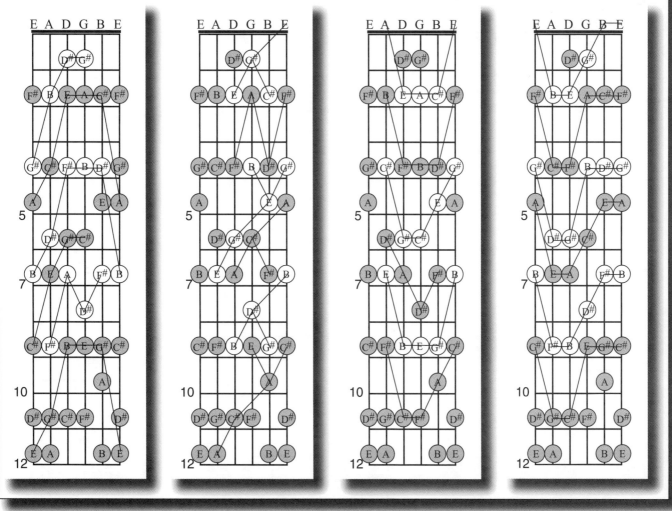

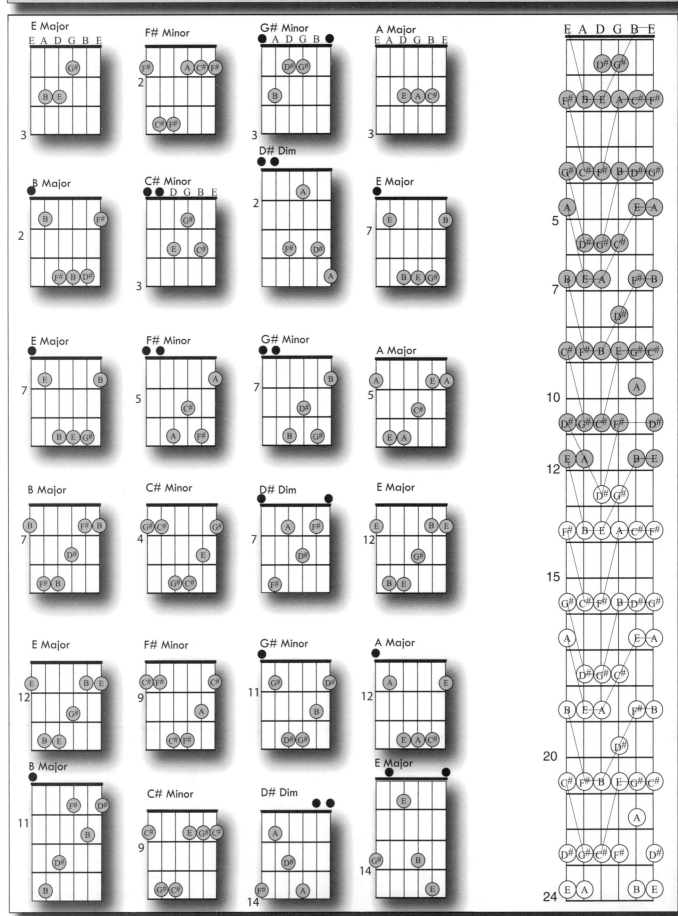

Seventh Chords

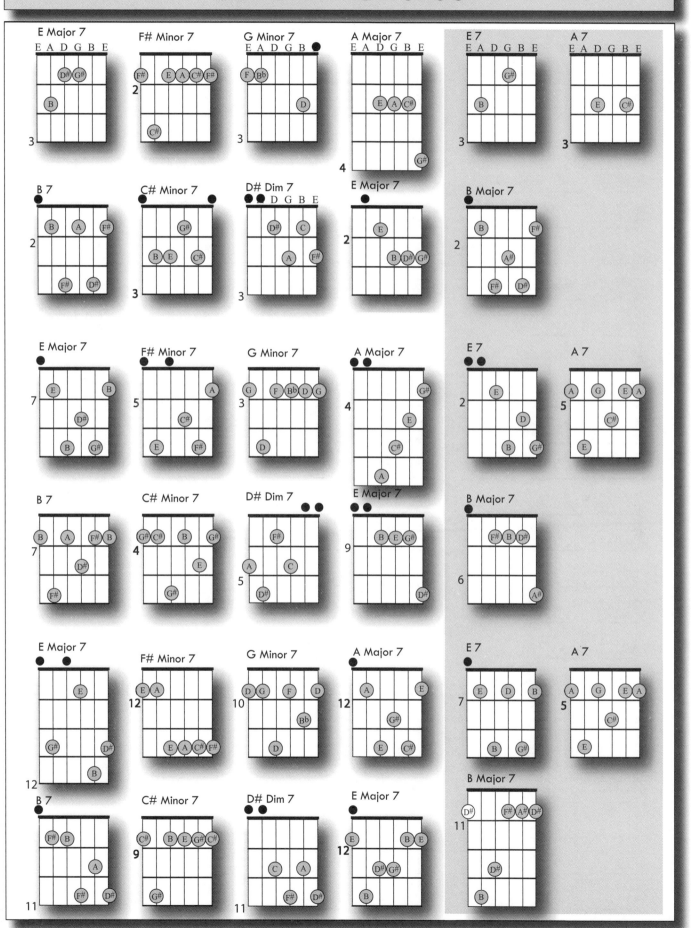

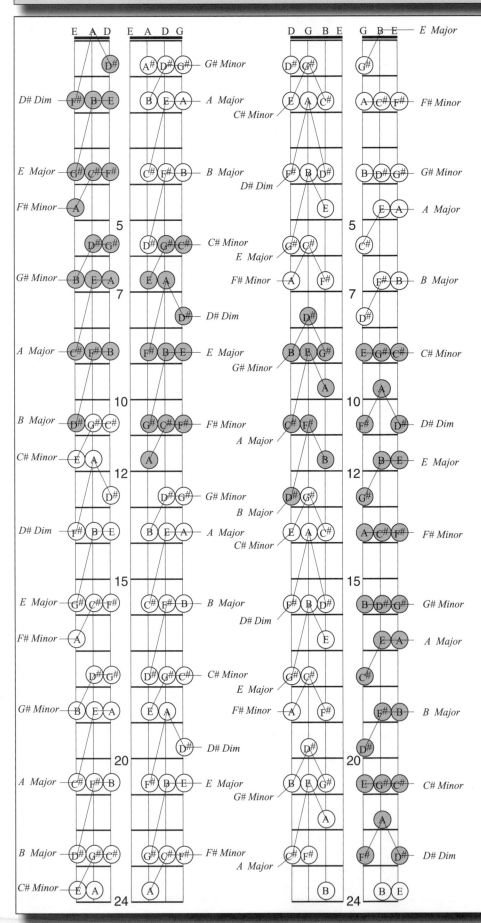

First Inversion Triads

Here is something to get you to think about the other inversions and the benefits of combining them.

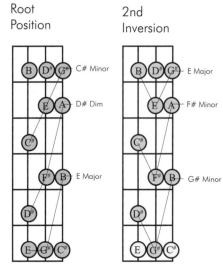

You can compare the different triads and probably find examples that would be very useful for your own needs.

Advanced Study

Pick a favorite progression of chords and try to find it using all three inversions. Look for ways to play it covering large stretches as well as ways to play it without moving to a new position.

Once you realize how versatile these different inversions are, you will find uses for it.

Second Inversion Triads

Here they are again.

1st Inversion

Root Position

As you play these chords, mix in the triads for the other positions. Try it with triads from other parts of the inversion. This is another way of learning and using the information.

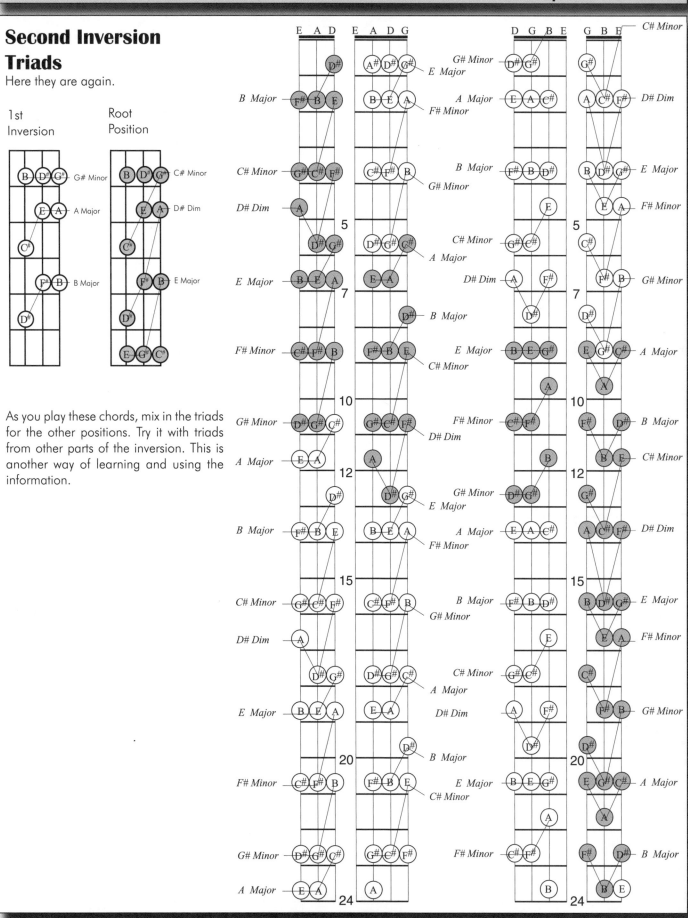

Root Inversion Triads For E Major

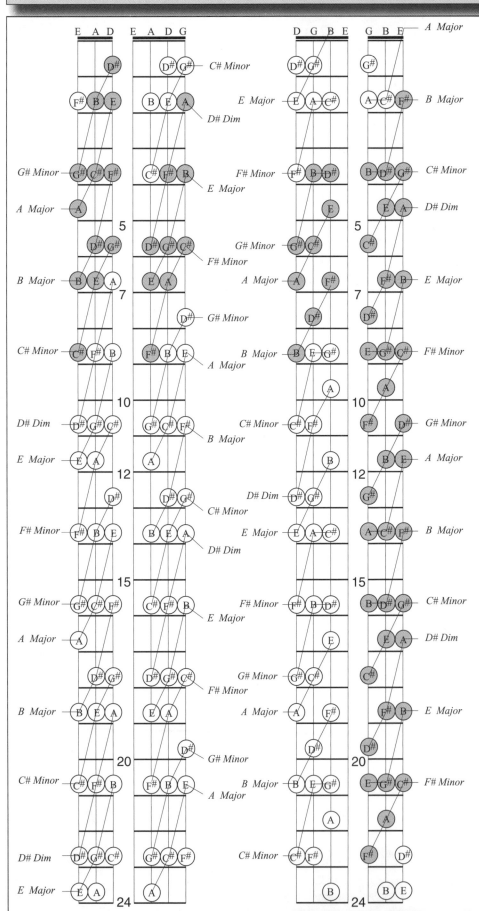

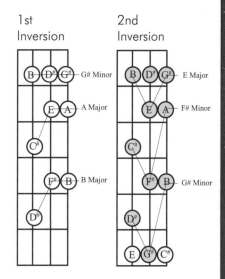

Root Position Triads

In a very limited space, we have shown the entire palette of basic chords for the key of E. As a general rule you should not have to go farther than four frets to play any chord you want. It may not be in the exact voicing you want, but it will be available in at least one form.

The Keys Of B Major And G# Minor

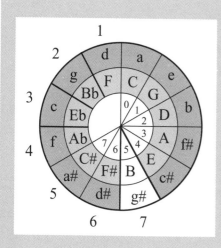

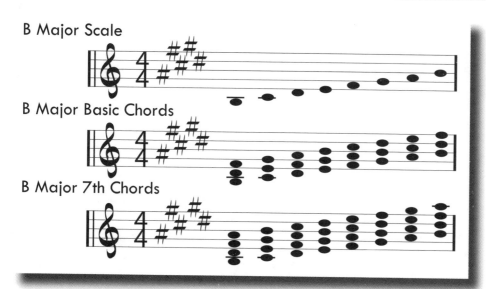

B Major Scale

B Major Basic Chords

B Major 7th Chords

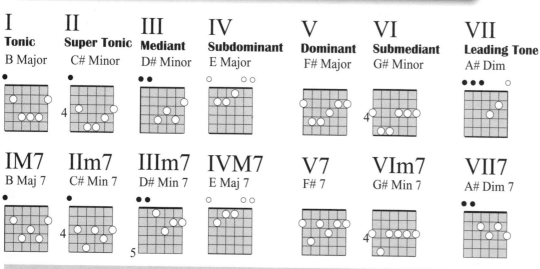

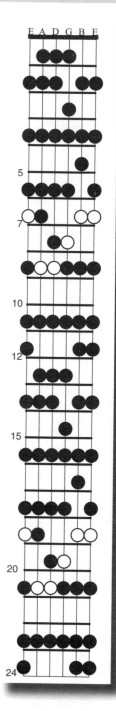

I	II	III	IV	V	VI	VII
Tonic	**Super Tonic**	**Mediant**	**Subdominant**	**Dominant**	**Submediant**	**Leading Tone**
B Major	C# Minor	D# Minor	E Major	F# Major	G# Minor	A# Dim

IM7	IIm7	IIIm7	IVM7	V7	VIm7	VII7
B Maj 7	C# Min 7	D# Min 7	E Maj 7	F# 7	G# Min 7	A# Dim 7

Typical Progressions

Another progression that comes to mind is the 1, 6, 2, 5, 1. It is worth discussing because 3 different arms of the graphic are employed. The supertonic is on one arm, the subdominant and submediant is on another arm and the dominant chord is on another arm. Musically this progression takes three different directions. Also, the leading tone chord can be substituted for the dominant to form a 1, 6, 2, 7, 1. Try it and see if it sounds acceptable as a substitution. See page 37.

Circular Or Linear

No matter how you look at it, the circle of fifth does the same thing. It describes how each key is situated in the big picture. It also describes the flats or sharps in each key and the differences from key to key. It can be more helpful to see the process as a linear diagram sometimes. But it is also helpful to see it as circular, because there is no beginning or end. It can help remind you that you must consider both the forward and backward relationships and that it works in a circular fashion.

We are also getting close to sharping all the notes. Notice that five of the notes are now sharped. We only have two notes left that are not sharped. But we will continue to add sharps as we go, and then something new will happen when we run out of notes to sharp.

When you look at the two diagrams together it can be easier to see how they both describe the motion of changing keys and the repetitious cycle of twelve interlocking keys. By the time we get to F major, the pattern will again be right next to C major and be in position to change the key and repeat the cycle. Each key changes it enough so that by the time twelve keys have passed, the circle appears as it did for the first key. We will explore this concept in the next key.

This is difficult to understand. We are adding sharps to each key and that changes the key. This way each key is unique, but they all adhere to the same rules. And if you follow the formula, you can easily create one key from another, and build any step in the process, as well as create an interlocking signature of notes that fully reflects the changes caused in each key. Confused? Talking about it without seeing an example makes it very difficult to understand. When you see it expressed physically over the course of several different keys, it will be easier to visualize.

The Interlocking Keys

Each key changes the numbers of sharps so it can maintain the same physical pattern and remain identical to the other keys. So at the same time a key is establishing a unique finger print, it is also conforming to the standard spacing of notes.

This works to create a unique interlocking set of keys that results in twelve tonal center.

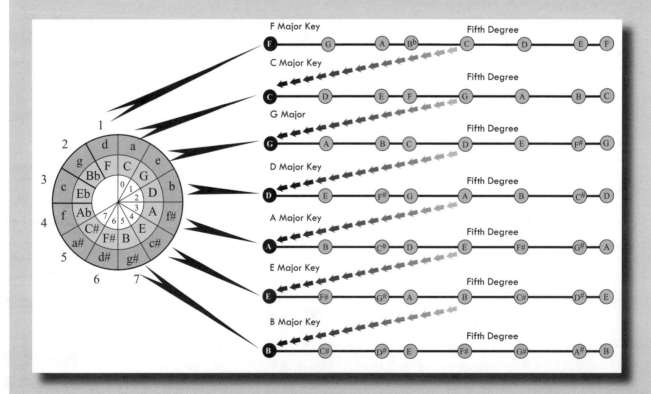

Chords Used In The Key

When you first look at the cascades below, you may not see all the different chords stuffed inside the signature. All these chords below are inside the signature and in place for the key of B major. These same forms will be used in all the other keys, only the location will be different. And the cascade remains intact when moving from key to key.

Some of these cascades, namely the first and fifth, contain parts of chords. The chords in these examples are not practical to play in their outlined form, but they are very useful when you are trying to borrow notes to create new configurations.

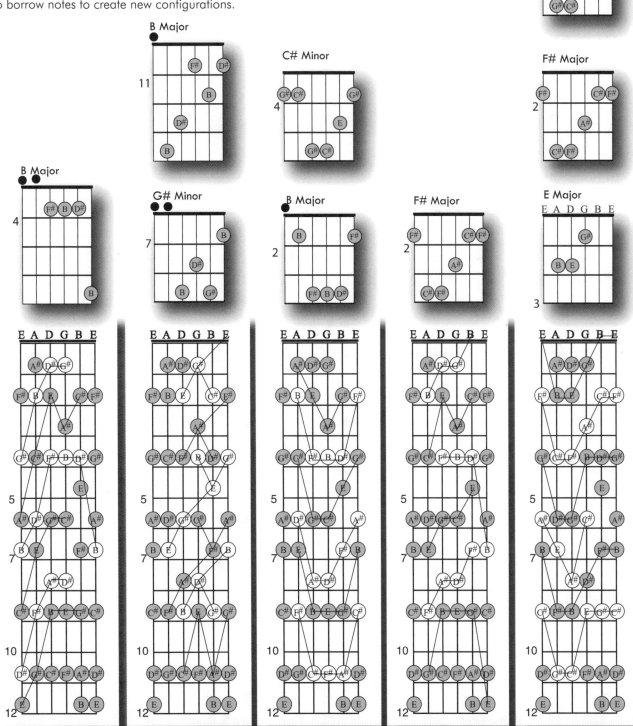

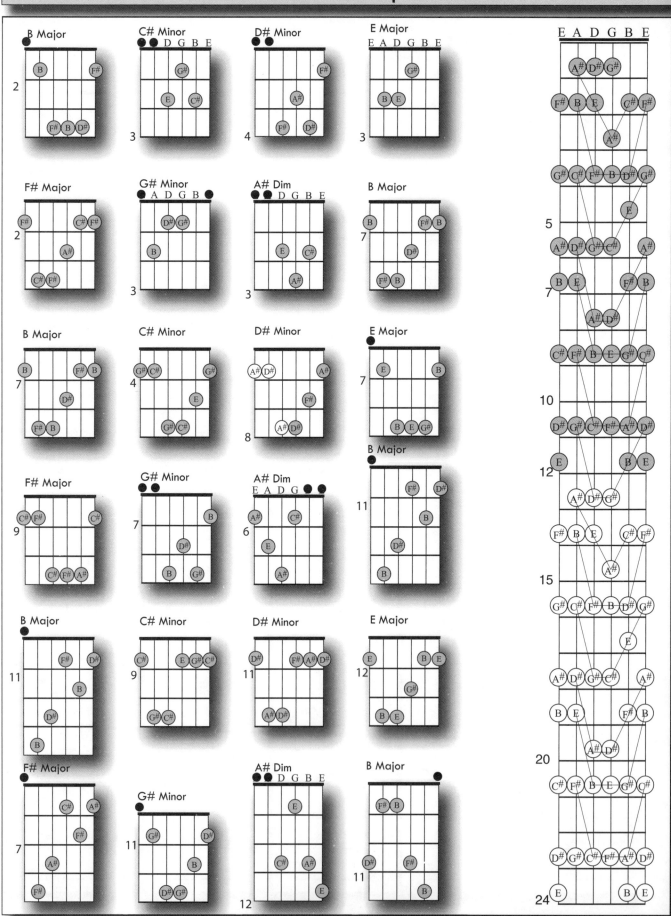

Seventh Chords

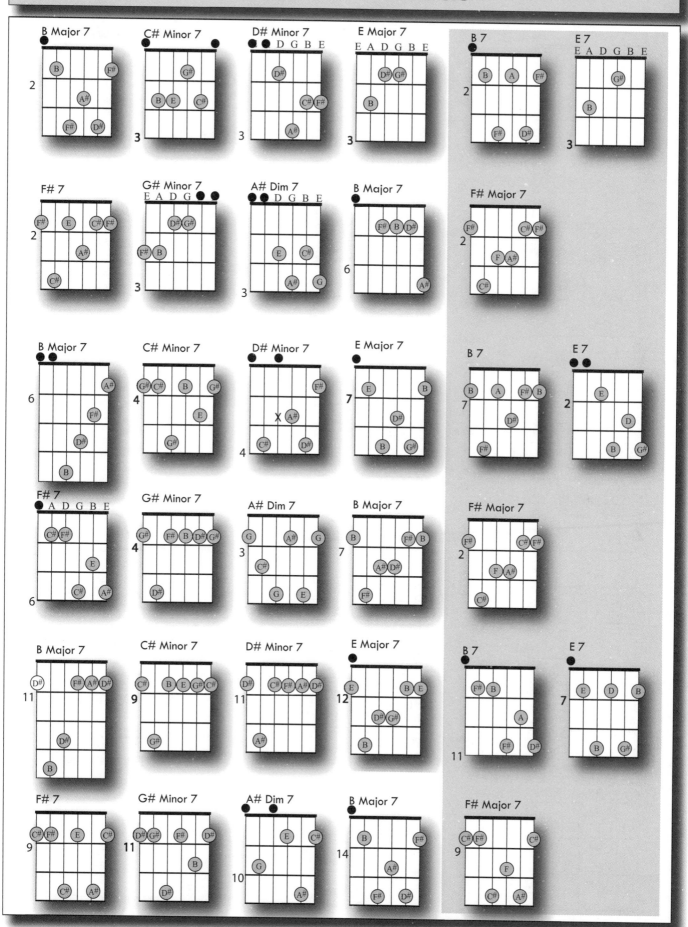

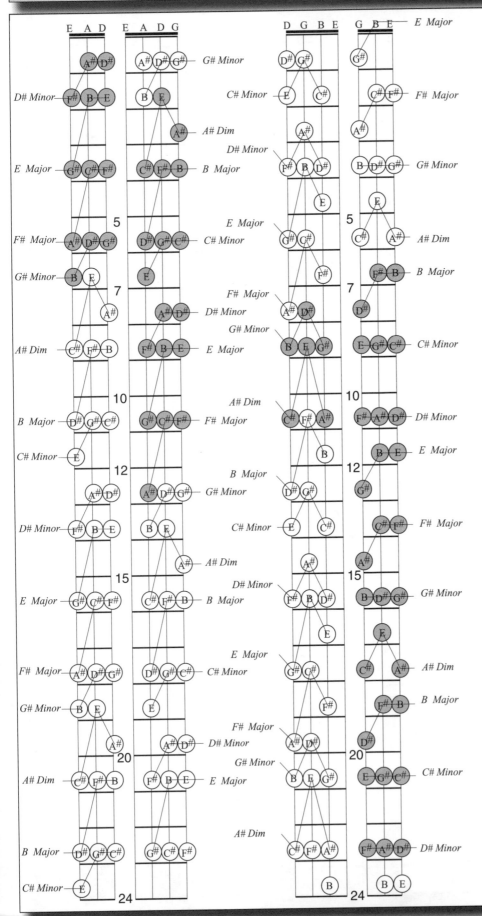

First Inversion Triads

There are five sharps in the key of B major but the triads look the same as other keys. The sharps are all accounted for by moving the pattern.

As you continue to play these chords, you will find some progressions have more meaning to you than others. You may like the sound or the movement between chords may provide an increase in confidence. Whatever the reason, it makes sense to realize why you like something. Identifying these moves or specific sounds can help you create a signature for your own style. That can be both good and bad. Signature moves are progressions or sounds that people can recognize as yours. This can also put you into a rut. A rut can occur when you get so comfortable with certain moves that they become too automatic. Instead of a creative outburst, you come up with the same moves.

That is one reason why, when you play these chords (as well as everything else), you work on using different fingers to play the chords. You will also want to try to approach the exercises from a fresh angle. Ruts will occur as you get more comfortable with what you are learning. They are not a bad thing as long as you recognize that you must work out of them by continuing to learn and apply these concepts.

First Inversion Triads

These triads are in the first inversion. The order of notes in the first inversion is 3, 5 and 1.

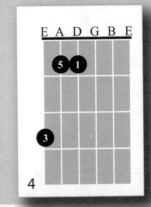

Second Inversion Triads

Notice that the second inversion chords also maintain the same forms for the major, minor and diminished triads. Pick a set of strings and examine all the major chords, then the minor chords and then the diminished chord.

This points out that the fretboard is quite orderly. If you get comfortable with the rules, you can expect the same results.

Advanced Study

By now you have heard the triads in relation to one another. You have no doubt heard the diminished triad and the transition to the tonic chord. The diminished triad is unique in that the distance between the first and fifth note is diminished. It is not a perfect fifth. Go back to the section about major and minor triads if you do not understand this. Because the distance is not a perfect fifth, the sound does not encourage you to stay on the chord for any length of time. In fact, when you play the scale of triads, there is a sense of urgency to get off the diminished triad and resolve the unsettled feeling by reaching tonic.

In practical application, the diminished chord is often referred to as a four note chord. Be careful because several different structures can be called a diminished chord. By definition a triad can only have three notes. So a four note chord cannot be accepted as a triad. You could however omit a degree of the chord and play the remaining three notes as a triad.

If you construct a four note chord remember for it to be diminished, all three thirds must be diminished. Keep in mind there are several different varieties of diminished chords. Although very valuable, the construction of these chords is beyond the scope of this book.

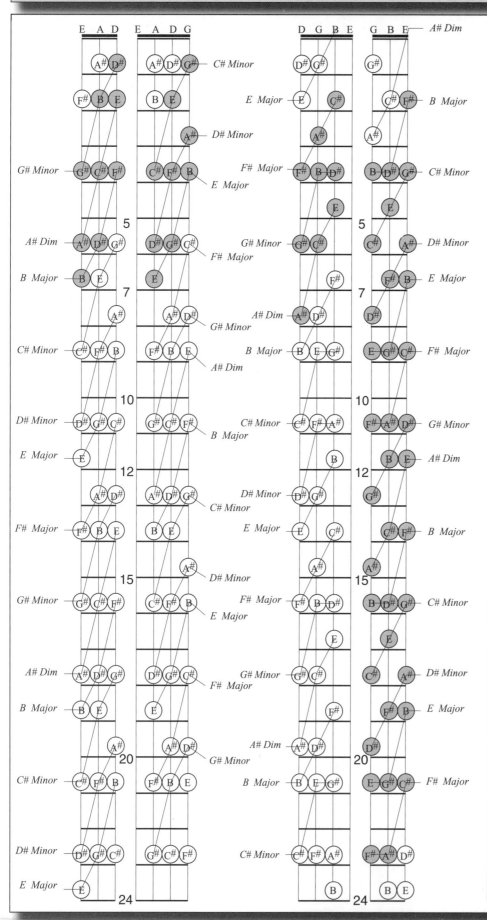

Root Position Triads

Why do we go through every key if these triads are the same? There are several good reasons. Repetition is essential to really learn the concepts well. There are many examples of repetition in these triads, but there are also many details and unique features to each key. In order to use the information on demand in a unique situation, you must be very familiar with these chords.

You must put yourself in a position to take advantage of what you know. This can take a while, and you may know them mentally before the physical comfort sets in. The result of this is that you know what to do, but still trip over the mechanics. Practice will take care of this and many other problems.

From time to time you may need to refer back to areas of interest or areas that remain foggy. This book will serve as a resource for referral after you memorize the information.

Root Inversion Triads

These triads are in the root position. The order of notes in the root inversion is 1, 3 and 5.

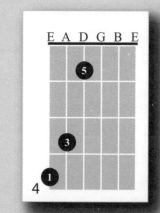

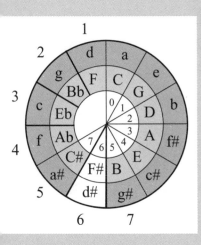

The Keys Of F# Major And D# Minor

F# Major Scale

F# Major Basic Chords

F# Major 7th Chords

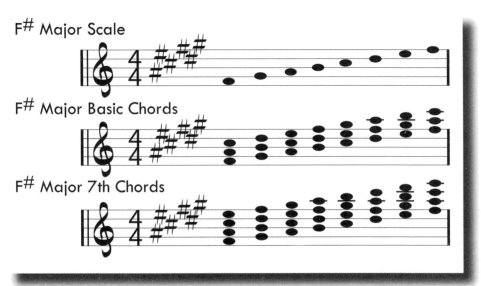

I	II	III	IV	V	VI	VII
Tonic	**Super Tonic**	**Mediant**	**Subdominant**	**Dominant**	**Submediant**	**Leading Tone**
F# Major	G# Minor	A# Minor	B Major	C# Major	D# Minor	E# Dim

IM7	IIm7	IIIm7	IVM7	V7	VIm7	VII7
F# Maj 7	G# Min 7	A# Min 7	B Maj 7	C# 7	D# Min 7	E# Dim 7

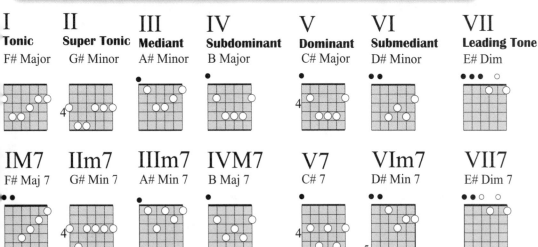

Relationship Between the 5th and 7th Degrees

Notes of the chords
Chord   1   3   5   7
C#   C#, E#, G# B
E#   E#, G#, B

Notice the E# has three identical notes of the C# chord if you play it as a seventh chord. This forms a very similar sound and the seventh degree chord (leading tone) can be substituted for the fifth degree chord (in this case the E# and C#). Do you see why the relationship exists?

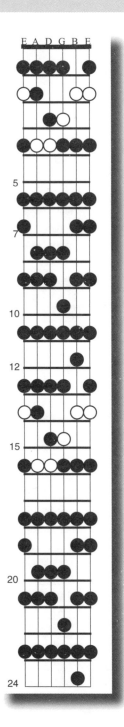

Changing The Physical Pattern To Form A New Key

Now we are arranging these twelve different signatures according to the ordering in the circle of fifths. Notice they seem to jump all around. The first six diagrams are the first six keys arranged chromatically, which makes it easy to see how each key is changed as we move the pattern.

These keys all use the same pattern and just move it up one fret to change all the relationships to conform to the new key. They proceed chromatically.

But the amount of sharps in each key varies wildly. C major has no sharps while the next key C# has seven sharps.

In the second set of signatures those relationships are now hidden. We are ordering these keys based on the circle of fifths and that means that every time we change to the next signature, the sharp count will increase by one. This way each new key changes based on the rules. It is important to be able to think about this both chromatically and by jumping five degrees at a time.

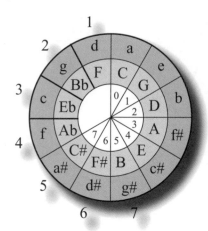

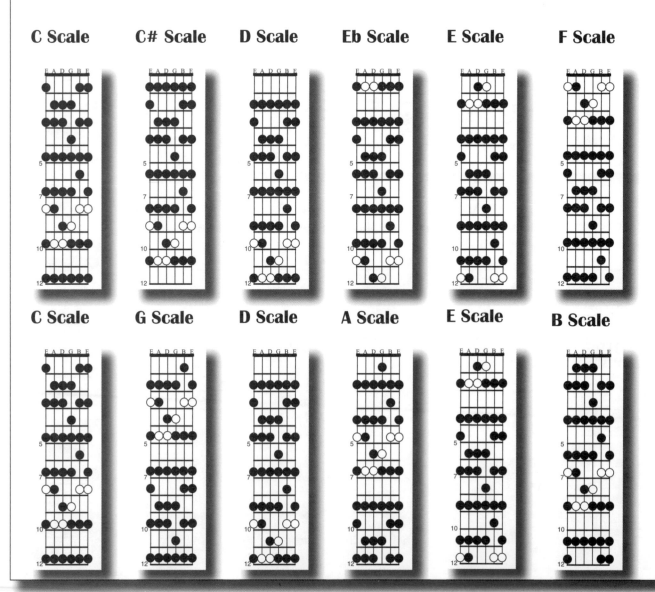

Working Chromatically Or By Five Degree Jumps

When we move by means of the circle of fifth, we are changing each key by adding a sharp to the seventh degree and carrying over the sharps from the previous keys. But the whole steps and half steps stay the same. Every time we add a new sharp we change the signature pattern. So each key changes the pattern.

Five Degree Jumps

The first example is how the keys look when we move by means of the circle of fifths and the five degree jump you take when constructing keys this way. By adding a sharp to the seventh degree of F major, we then change the scale to become C major. We will have covered twelve keys by the time we get to F major and every time we will add a sharp to the seventh degree to make the key unique. And as soon as we do it for the 13th time, we end up creating the key of C major again and so we have now completed one trip around the circle. This formula for creating keys has caused us to recreate the key of C.

Moving Chromatically

But when we move chromatically we jump up to the next note and construct the next key by starting on the keynote and placing notes according to the whole step, whole step, half step, whole step, whole step, whole step, half step rule. Each key uses the same pattern, because it is constructed according to the same rules of whole steps and half steps. After you move this pattern twelve times, you arrive at the key of C major again.

One way you travel by five degree jumps and start repeating every twelve keys and the other way you move chromatically and after twelve frets, you repeat the process. There are only twelve possible different keys according to the rules of diatonic keys. No matter if you work visually or construct keys according to the traditional rules of music theory, you still get the same thing. The twelve keys are very tightly integrated and it can be simple to look at a picture and understand the relationships.

F Scale **C Scale**
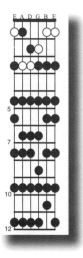 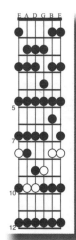

B Scale **C Scale**
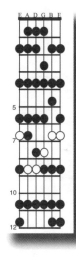 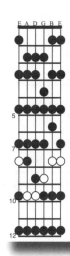

F# Scale   **C# Scale**   **Ab Scale**   **Eb Scale**   **Bb Scale**   **F Scale**

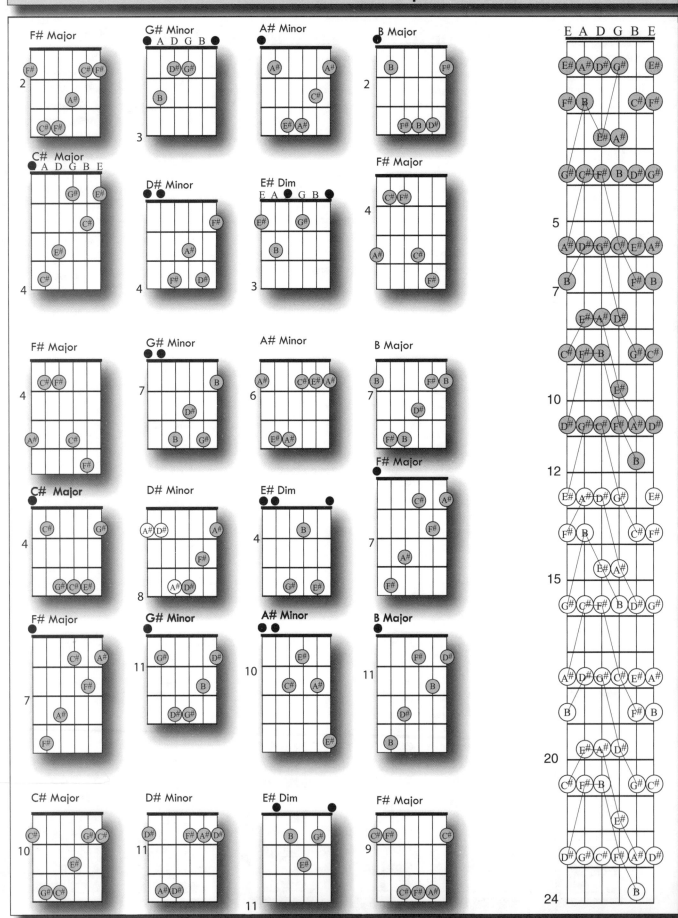

Seventh Chords

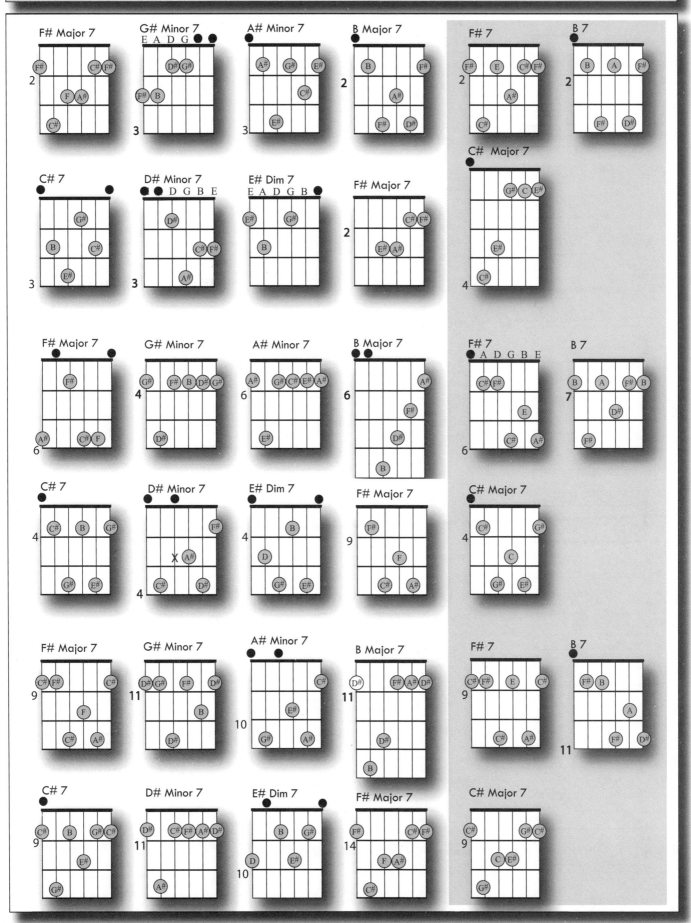

1st Inversion Triads For F# Major

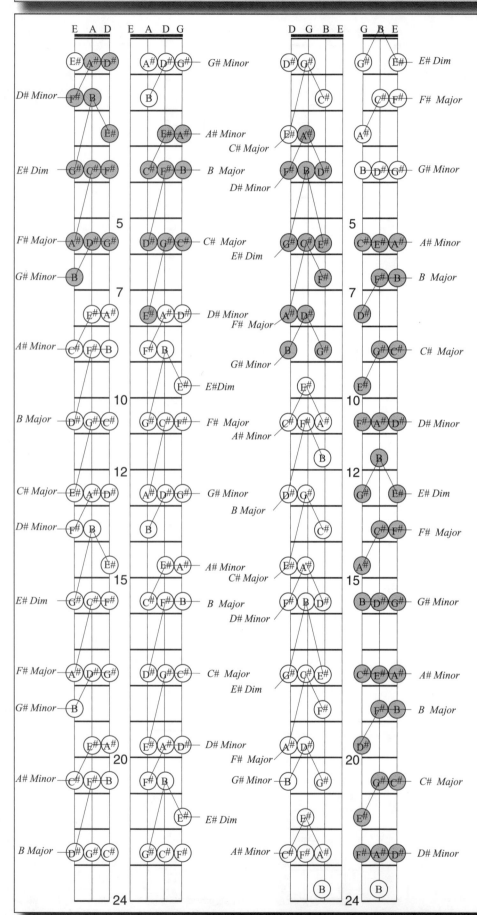

First Inversion Triads

Here is the standard third, fifth and first degrees of the scale. Start on the note of the F# scale for which you are building a chord. Starting on that note and naming it as the first degree, follow the scale to the third note and then the fifth note. The starting note will name the chord, the third and fifth note will define the type of chord it is. For a major key, there are three types of naturally occurring triads . They are the major, minor and the diminished triads.

Advanced Study

Take time to construct several of these chords on your own to observe the rules in action. It is very valuable to actually change this scale for the next key and construct the chords before you see them.

From this key to the next, three chords will change. F# contains six sharps. The F, G, A, C, D and E are sharped. The chords generated are on this page. The next key is the C#. It has the same sharps as F# and it adds a B#. Every triad that has a B will now be sharped and will change. The first example is the E# dim. From G# to B is a minor third. By sharping the B it is now a major third and changes from a diminished chord to a minor chord.

The next example is the G# minor. From G# to B is a minor third and the chord is a minor chord. By sharping the B, the third is now a major third and so is the chord. The next example is the B major, which will become a B# diminished. By sharping the B you change the lower third into a minor third. The chord now has two minor thirds and is now a diminished chord. If you had trouble following that, go back to the section where major, minor, diminished and augmented chords are defined. We went through that quickly. Go back and construct the entire triad if you do not see how the changes affect the chord. You can look at the next key as you read this too.

Second Inversion Triads

Remember to play the triads slowly. Make sure each note is sounding without buzzing or muting another string. Each note should be played directly behind the fret. Do not move to the next chord until each one is played correctly. Do not allow bad habits to continue. Actively examine your technique and remove any less than desirable habits that show up.

Advanced Study

The examples cited for the first inversion will apply for the other inversions, too. The rules affect all chords regardless of the stacking.

An interesting thing is about to occur. At the next stop on the Circle of Fifths, we will add another sharp. That means all the notes will be sharped. How then will we differentiate the next key? Remember enharmonic spellings? Rather than spell the key by reciting seven sharps, we will flip all the notes from sharps to flats and describe them by the flatted spelling.

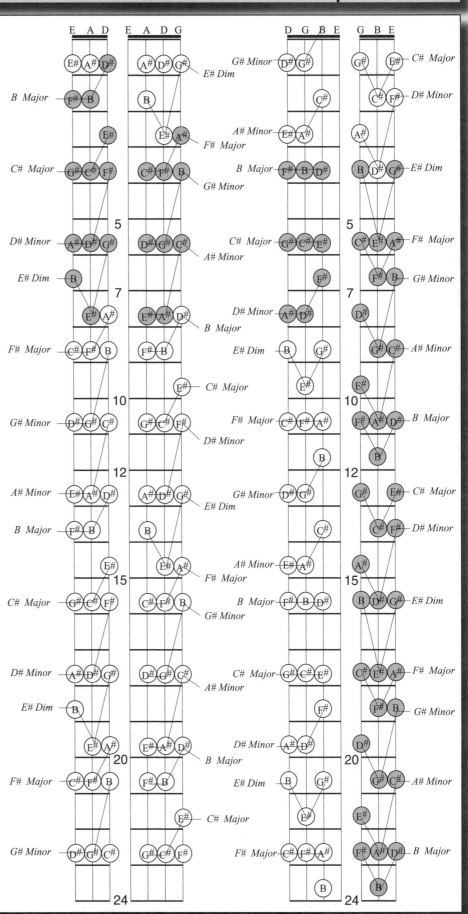

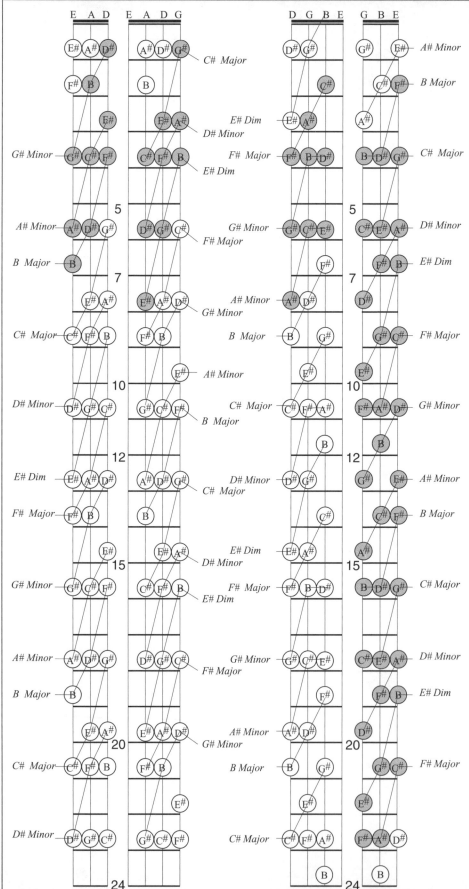

Root Position Triads

Have you examined where your thumb is situated when you play these triads. The thumb on your left hand (the one that is on the fretboard) should be right below your second finger. It should also be riding in the middle of the back of the neck. A common bad habit is to wrap the neck with the thumb (sometimes in an effort to apply more pressure). By keeping the thumb right below the second finger, it decreases your reaction time to switch notes and play the next chord. There is a difference in the exact muscles used when the thumb is out of position. If you wrap the neck, you will have a little trouble playing with your thumb right below the second finger. When you learn these triads, try to keep an eye on your hand position. It can make a significant difference as you add more skills. For a complete reference of technique, consult Uncle Tim's First Year.

D# Minor The Relative Minor

Here is a little trick to see if your mind can spot the relative minor chord as you pass by it. Play the triads in order using any path you want. Play the sequence several times up and down the fretboard climbing at least one and one half octaves. Without looking or thinking about the names of the chords you are playing, try to identify the relative minor as you come across it in the sequence. Two things happen as you do this. First you might be in tune with the relative major and be fixed in that key. If so, you might not feel the relative minor bring the sequence to rest. You might just think it asks to be resolved by means of major tonic.

The second thing that may happen is that you recognize the more subtle resolution by means of the relative minor. You may hear and respond by stopping on that chord. Try running the relative minor scale over these chords too.

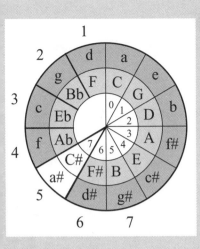

The Keys Of C# Major And A# Minor

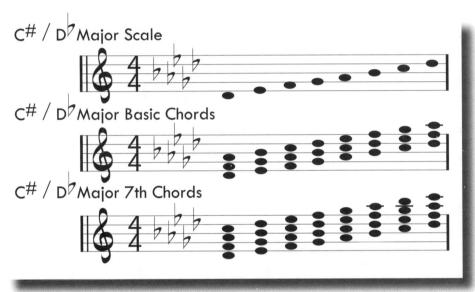

C# / D♭ Major Scale

C# / D♭ Major Basic Chords

C# / D♭ Major 7th Chords

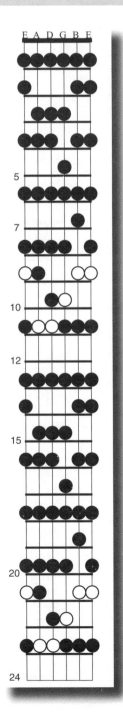

I	II	III	IV	V	VI	VII
Tonic	**Super Tonic**	**Mediant**	**Subdominant**	**Dominant**	**Submediant**	**Leading Tone**
C# Major	D# Minor	E# Minor	F# Major	G# Major	A# Minor	B# Dim

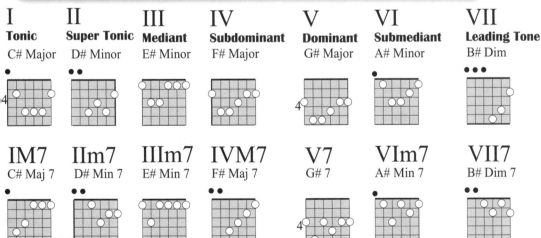

IM7	IIm7	IIIm7	IVM7	V7	VIm7	VII7
C# Maj 7	D# Min 7	E# Min 7	F# Maj 7	G# 7	A# Min 7	B# Dim 7

Substitutions

Primary chords are listed as the one, four and five chords. Secondary chords include the two, three, six and seventh degrees. These secondary chords can be substituted for the primary chords and will add interest. Try substituting the three for the fifth degree chord, the two for the fourth and the seventh for the fifth as discussed previously.
Here is a breakdown

2 chord	Eb, <u>Gb, Bb</u>
4 chord	<u>Gb, Bb</u>, Db
3 chord	F, <u>Ab, C</u>
5 chord	<u>Ab, C</u>, Eb

C# Is One Fret Higher Than C

When we change keys from C major to C# major, we will have added sharps to every note. They are now all sharped. There are a couple of interesting things to notice right here.

The key of C major has no sharps. The key of C# has 7 sharps. It is just like C major except everything is one half step higher. Look at the diagram to the right and notice the key of C and C# are identical except in C#, everything is sharped. This is a good example of how the physical fretboard exactly reflects the laws of diatonic keys.

The implication is, not only does the pattern adhere to the rules of music but all the chords in both examples are identical as are the scales. The benefit is everything you know in the key of C major can be transferred to this key by sharping it (moving it up one fret). If you put a capo on the first fret and you play a C major chord, you are actually playing a C# major chord. The capo changed the tuning of the guitar by raising it one half step.

This is one of the biggest tools I have ever encountered. Being able to translate everything into another key at will provides very big benefits. An obvious benefit is you can easily know all your scales for every key. This is itself a major accomplishment. Another benefit is that you can grasp the concepts behind chords and key and understand how they flow across the fretboard. This puts a person in the position to command chords and scales together. A serious guitarist should be able to find considerable use for these skills.

C Scale   **C# Scale**

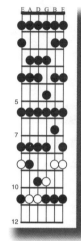

So make sure you are working in different keys and taking advantage of the full benefit of your hard work.

Enharmonic Spellings

C# and Db are the same thing. Here is the physical signature for the key of C# major. Both diagrams are identical musically. There is no difference at all. The first example illustrates the key of C# major, in sharps. Look closely and you will see all the notes are sharped. Every sharp note on the fretboard is present. No natural notes are present.

The second fretboard is the same key of C# major, only now it is expressed in flats. Remember a B# is actually a C note. Notice this fretboard does not contain any sharps, but the signature of C# major is unmistakable. The dots are all in the same place as the first example. Also notice that although there are some flats present, there are also some natural notes present. There are only five flat note possible. B# and E# can both be described as the natural notes C and F respectively.

The only way you can describe a C and F as flats is to describe them as double flats (bb), and that is what we will look at next.

Flipping The key

Usually this is the point when we stop talking about the present key in terms of sharps and start talking about it in terms of flats.

The key of C# is called C# most of the time but sometimes it is referred to as Db. The next key is almost always referred to as Ab. I never hear it called G# major.

Being able to think in terms of sharps and flats is very important and difficult. So I find the visual aid indispensable. I almost always need a fretboard with both spellings present when working out difficult concepts.

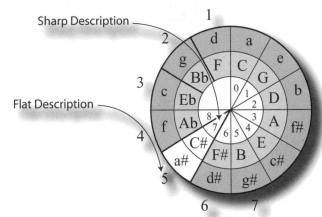

Notice the outside number is the number of flats present in the key. The inside number is the number of sharps in the key. The inside numbers stop at C# while the outside numbers extend to the key of B major. You can continue both sets of numbers around the circle if you want, but usually these are the ones shown and used.

Too Many Sharps Gets Confusing

As we stated earlier, using sharps when notating these keys can be quite confusing. There are just too many of them on the staff. The next key is going to introduce another sharp which will cause even more clutter, so rather than using all these sharps, we express the key using flats, and it instantly becomes manageable.

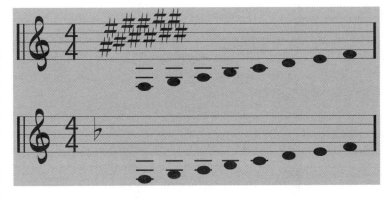

The graphic below is the same one that appeared earlier. We are describing the key of F major and we are using sharps in the first example and flats in the second. A similar thing happens when we look at the physical signature only it is not this extreme. Most written music that you will encounter will adhere to this convention.

Seven Sharps And The Next Key Will Add Another One

So far every key has added a sharp as a new key is created. You know we are going to do the same thing at the next key, Ab. The construction process will continue unaltered. The rules do not change even through we have applied sharps to all the notes, we are just going to add them to notes already sharped.

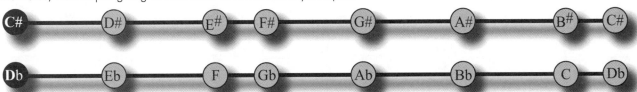

Everything Works Together

Everything we have used to discuss music, either notation, the circle of fifths, the sound of a key or a physical description all serve to describe the rules of diatonic keys. They all describe the same thing. Each one has a benefit to using it as well as a weakness. Together they help a person to see all sides of musical issues and if you pick the right tool, the answer will jump out at you. They all have a purpose. They all work together and they are all tools you can rely on.

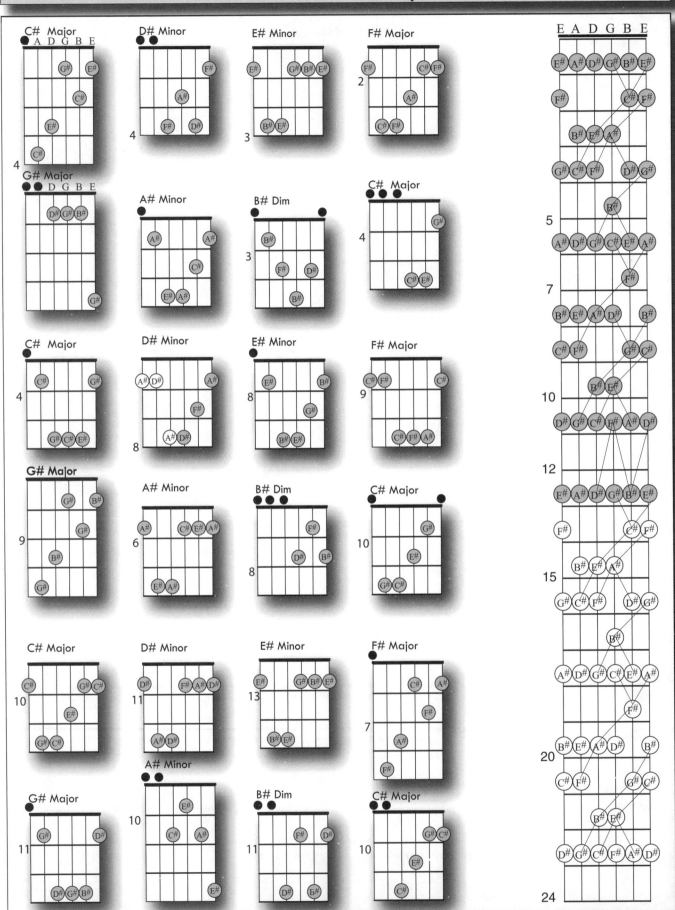

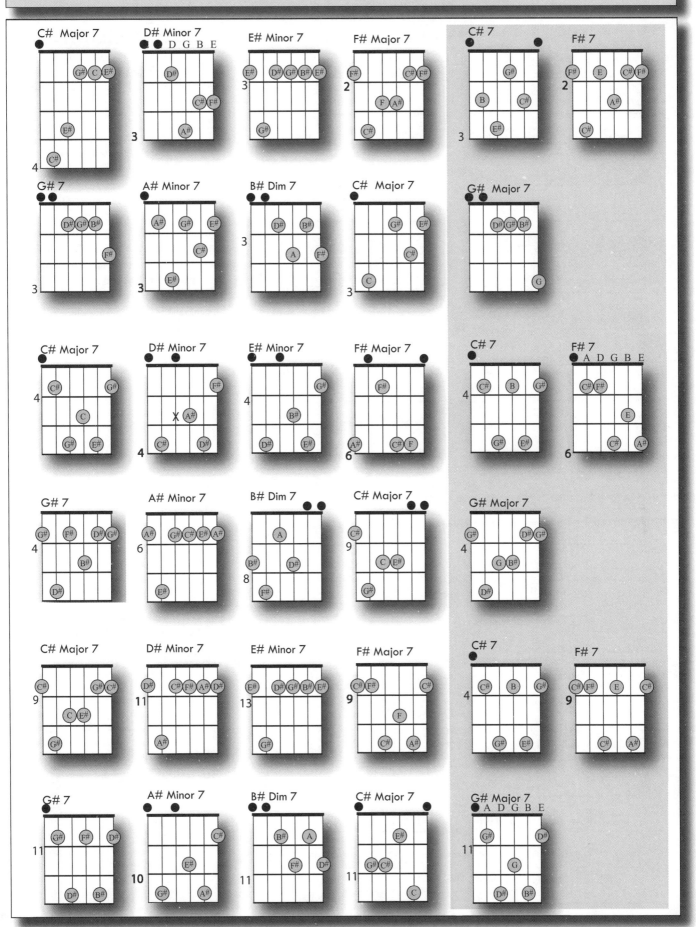

1st Inversion Triads For C# Major

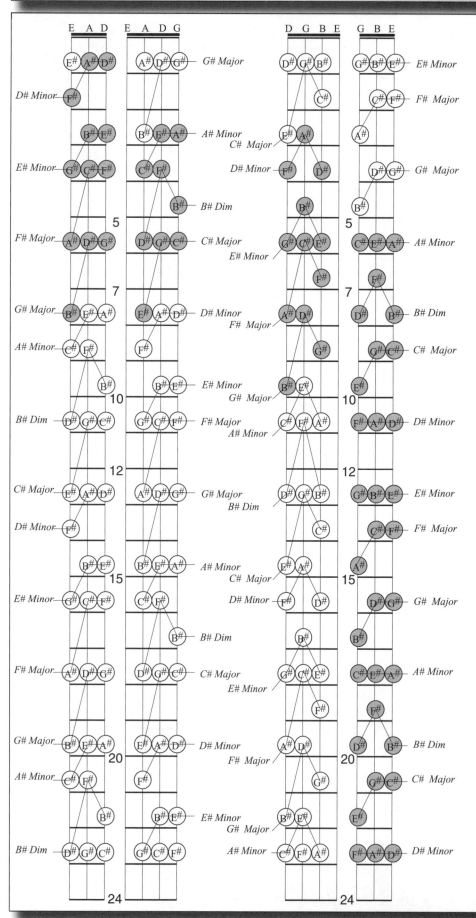

First Inversion Triads

Don't look for any open strings to go with these chords. This key has seven sharps. Notice that the triads get started at the first fret. This key is one fret above the key of C. The simplicity at the neck has been lost because there are no open strings to work with as in the key of C.

Other than the open strings, there is no difference between the C and Db pattern. It is also a good idea to play the triads for the key of C and then play this key. Because the keys are so close, it can be easier to identify the relationships in the pattern if you examine them chromatically.

First Inversion Triads

These triads are in the first inversion. The order of notes in the first inversion is 3, 5 and 1.

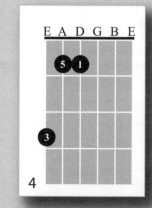

Second Inversion Triads

The second inversion provides the typical D major and D minor forms as seen on the three highest strings. Notice that both of these chord forms are shown on the first page of Common Chords in The Scale (page 26-28).

Also notice that the triads shown on this page will only show the primary notes (1, 3 and 5). However, these common chords have additional notes attached. Also notice that the attached notes are one of the three degrees used in the triad construction.

Most of these triads show up in common chords. They are very usable as a mechanism for chord construction. This can be helpful when you are building secondary parts for a new song. If you know the chords of the song, alternate fingerings of notes can be accomplished by consulting the different inversions of these triads. If you are working in Db major and you need to supply a change or new direction for the music, use these triads as a palette. If you are looking for a few notes to help you accent the change between chords, the scale for each key will provide the palette of notes for any passage based on a diatonic key.

Advanced Study

Keep in mind that there are times when you will want to violate the concept of tonal construction. In those cases, you would use notes other than the ones presented in the scale. A diminished seventh chord can be an example of that. It is common to see this chord expressed as a four note chord that uses the first, third, fifth and seventh notes. When you use a flatted seventh degree, you are violating the pattern because the flatted seventh is not in the diatonic pattern. The 7th is flatted in this chord so that all three thirds are minor. Remember two minor thirds form a minor chord, three minor thirds form a diminished seventh chord.

More on this later.

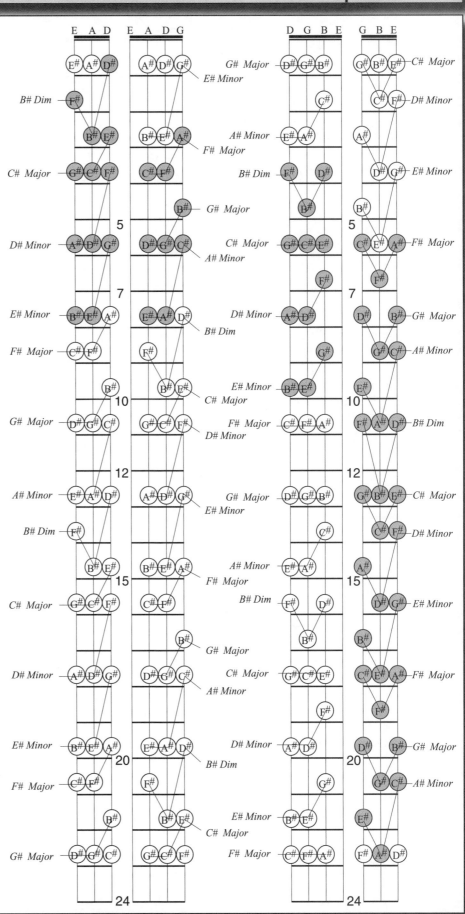

Root Inversion Triads For C# Major

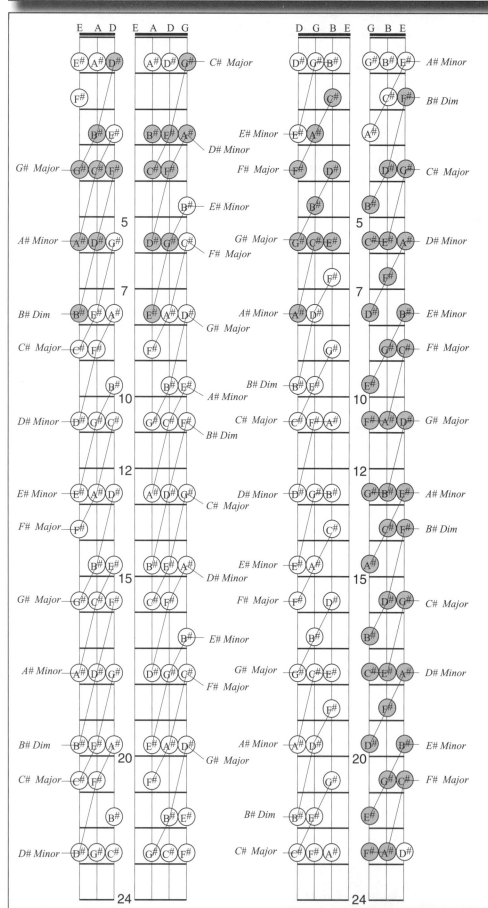

Root Position Triads

Run these chords by playing them all on the same three strings, and then run them by climbing one octave and moving across the fretboard.

Notice the chord is the same but the sound is slightly different.

There are two things I want to point out. First, there are two ways to travel and play these chords, vertically and horizontally. Look back to the page, Movement on The Fretboard (page 20).

The second thing I want to point out is something you are probably aware of. The strings are constructed differently and will give off a distinct sound for each string. You have to pay attention to notice the difference but the sound of each string is different. This will affect how a chord will sound.

An obvious example would be to play the Gb major chord using the lowest three strings and then play it using the A, D and G strings. The second chord will be the same pitch because each note is the same pitch. Look it up on the scale and start comparing octaves. If you still do not see it, play it on a guitar and listen to the pitch.

So the pitch is the same but the chords sound slightly different. The difference is in the characteristics of the strings. Four strings are usually wound and two are not wound. By winding the string and increasing the thickness, a deeper bass sound is created.

You can hear the difference when you tune the guitar by playing the A note on the fifth fret of the low E string and matching the pitch on the open A string.

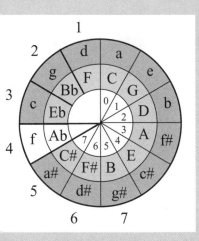

The Keys Of A♭ Major And F Minor

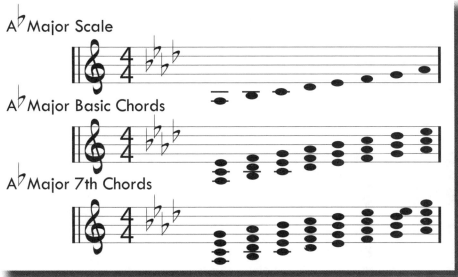

A♭ Major Scale

A♭ Major Basic Chords

A♭ Major 7th Chords

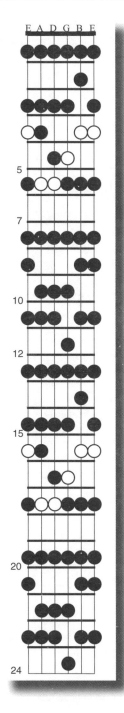

I	II	III	IV	V	VI	VII
Tonic	**Super Tonic**	**Mediant**	**Subdominant**	**Dominant**	**Submediant**	**Leading Tone**
Ab Major	Bb Minor	C Minor	Db Major	Eb Major	F Minor	G Dim

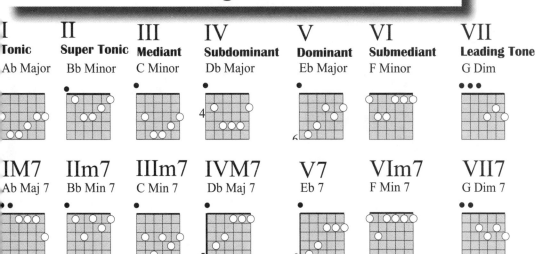

IM7	IIm7	IIIm7	IVM7	V7	VIm7	VII7
Ab Maj 7	Bb Min 7	C Min 7	Db Maj 7	Eb 7	F Min 7	G Dim 7

Extensions

You can change any chord by including an extension to the first, third and fifth degrees. For instance you could include a fourth degree, so you would play the first, third, fourth, and fifth. You can also omit certain notes to suit your own needs. Many times this additional note will be hammered on or pulled off to give a hint of movement. Any note can be added as an extension as long as it is in the scale.

The key of Ab

This key is the first one expressed as a flat key. But everything works the same way. The fifth degree of C# is G#, which of course is an Ab. So Ab becomes the new key and we are going to sharp the seventh degree of the new scale to create this key.

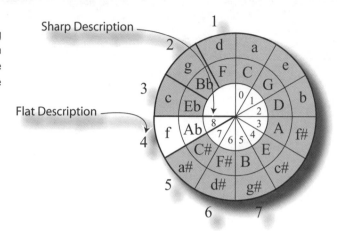

Enharmonic Spelling For Ab / G#						
Ab	Bb	C	Db	Eb	F	G
G#	A#	B#	C#	D#	E#	F##

The Double Sharp

So as usual we added a sharp to the seventh degree of the scale. In this case the note before we sharped it was an F#. Now the new note is an F##. An F## is the same thing as a G note. If you are at F and you sharp the note twice, you move two frets up to the G note. So now we have six sharps and a double sharp. Notice there is now a number 8 in the sharp description for Ab because there are eight sharps in the key. Usually this is not shown, but it helps to illustrate this concept.

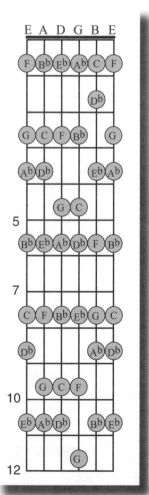

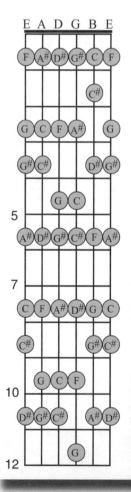

Enharmonic Spelling For Ab / G#

You can see both spellings describe the same key but I would not expect to see the second example in use much. It makes sense to look at this but express the key the same way as everyone else. It will be easier if you read some sheet music outlining a song or if you have to mix certain chord parts with a lead line because anything written will probably be in the flat spelling.

Transposing back and forth can get old. It is worth knowing how to do it, but most of us would rather spend that time playing.

Another consideration is what happens when you start describing advanced tonal centers or scales. At times, when using exotic scale signatures, it is not possible to express some scales by using just sharps or flats. You will need to mix them to accurately describe the scale. So getting to know the basics of enharmonic spellings will pay benefits once the skill is learned.

So for the rest of the keys we will use flats when constructing and describing keys. Take a look at the circle of fifths and notice that this key has four flats in it. The next key has three flats in it and the one after that has two flats. The last key, F major has one flat in it and C major has no flats in it.

You can describe any key in terms of flats or sharps. Sometimes it makes sense to do it, other times it does not.

At this point hopefully the process of working through the circle of fifths will start to seem logical. We have seen nine keys use the exact same formula to identify their respective keys. Nothing will change as we apply these construction techniques to the remaining keys.

If you have been playing and following the text, you are learning on a variety of levels. You are learning how to play the chords as well as learning how they are created. You are getting your arms around the world of diatonic keys and from that activity, a deeper understanding will develop.

Develop A Learning Cycle

As you play this material, you get better. As you get better, you develop more control. As you develop more control, you begin to really like it. All of these things make the other areas better. They all affect each other and over time, a repeating pattern of learning sets up, just like a machine. The by-product of this machine is increased control over the instrument which means you play better.

Understanding On Two Levels

Learning and playing the guitar can be broken into two separate parts.

Short term learning is the process of learning new concepts and committing them to memory. It only takes a short burst of intense work to memorize something.

Long term learning is the process of using the knowledge to do something. You may memorize chords right away, but your understanding of them takes far longer to develop.

The same thing applies to the circle of fifths. You now know how it works and if pressed, you could probably use it to recreate all these chords. In as early as a few months you will be using it to craft songs. This information will continue to affect your ability to play the guitar for a long time.

The cycle of learning produces a by-product of greater control and more ability. If you continue to practice, the machine will continue to provide you with better skills. This is a very significant benefit to continued structured practice.

In the next key, we will look at practicing.

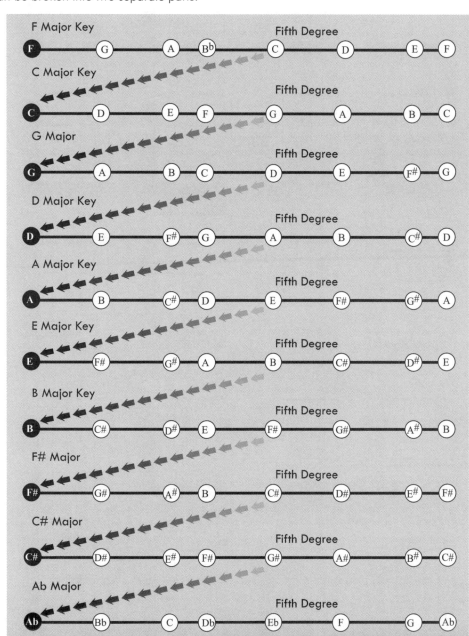

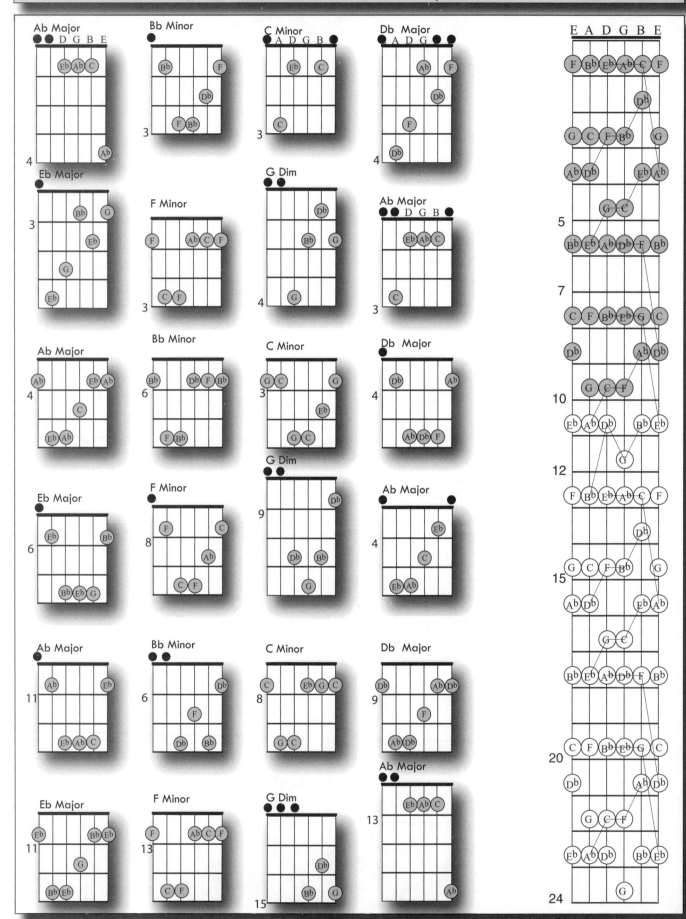

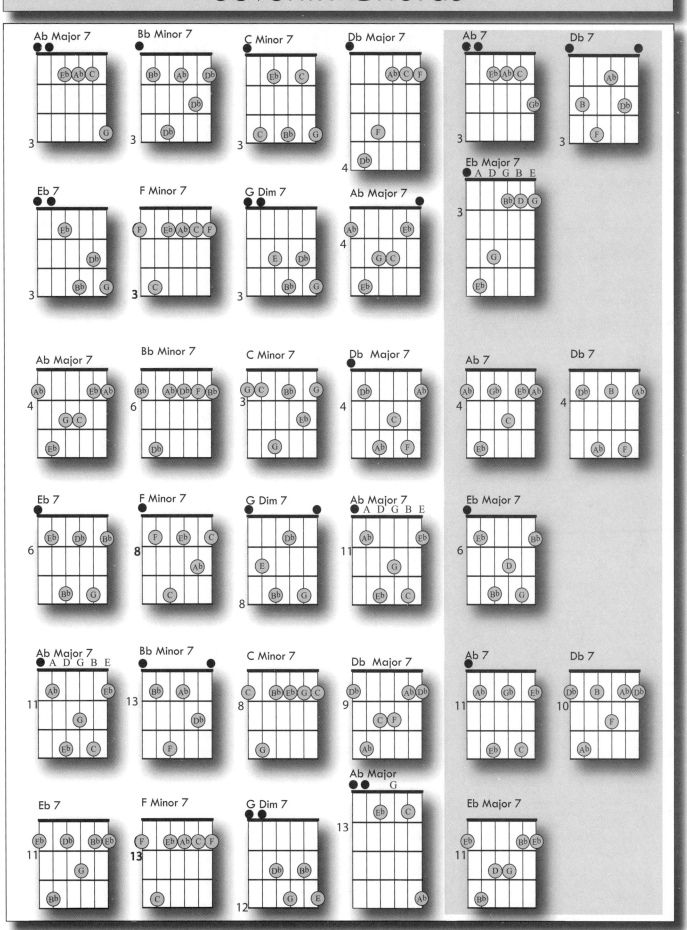

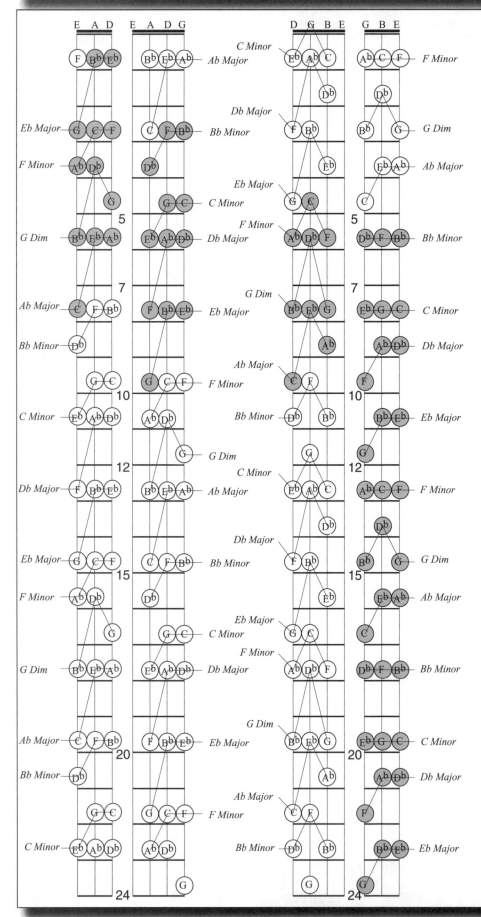

First Inversion Triads

Remember to play the chords slowly! Be precise with your movements between chords and concentrate on creating good tone. Are strings buzzing? Are you muting some notes? Are they all sounding correctly? Do you feel strength building in your hands? Remember at first, you could only play for a short while before fatigue would set in? Now you should be able to play for a longer period before fatiguing. These are signs that you are learning this information. Hopefully, you are experiencing these and other signs that this information is gaining meaning.

Are you starting to recognize the same chords are used for every key? By now, you are probably getting comfortable with the tonic chords and the difference between chords in the key. Have you noticed that the diminished sounds correct, but is not a chord you would use to bring a piece to rest. You naturally want to continue to the tonic note which is just above it. By playing the chords in a standard progression, you can feel the natural tendency of chords to relate to one another differently.

Also notice that this deep into the circle of fifths there are no open string-notes that can be combined to add interest to these chords. Although you could play an open G note with the G diminished chord, there are no other chords to use an open string with. Certainly there are no open strings that can be played with an entire set of chords. The reason is that the notes of the open strings are not in the scale for the key (with the exception of G).

Second Inversion Triads

Here is an interesting relationship to notice. Look at the chords for the highest three strings. Now choose just one note for a chord, and compare it to the same note for the next chord.

Do you notice that the notes happen sequentially? In other words, the first degree for each chord will progress Db, then the Eb, then F, etc...

Each note is followed by the next note in the series. All notes in the scale are used as you construct the triads for the key. This is evident when you look at the pages for Triads In The Pattern. It is easier to see that the triads are sandwiched right next to one another. Just remember, when you play these triads in order, you are playing three note scales.

F Minor
The Relative Minor

If you are working only in the major keys, you are not taking total advantage of this information.

Along with playing these chords as they relate to the relative minor, try some progressions transposed to the relative minor key. Start with the easy chords like the 1, 5 and 4 chords played in some order.

Then experiment with mixing different chords in the key to try to develop some feeling for the relative minor. It pays off. Often times the benefits of playing in a key are not apparent until you commit some time and play on the playground.

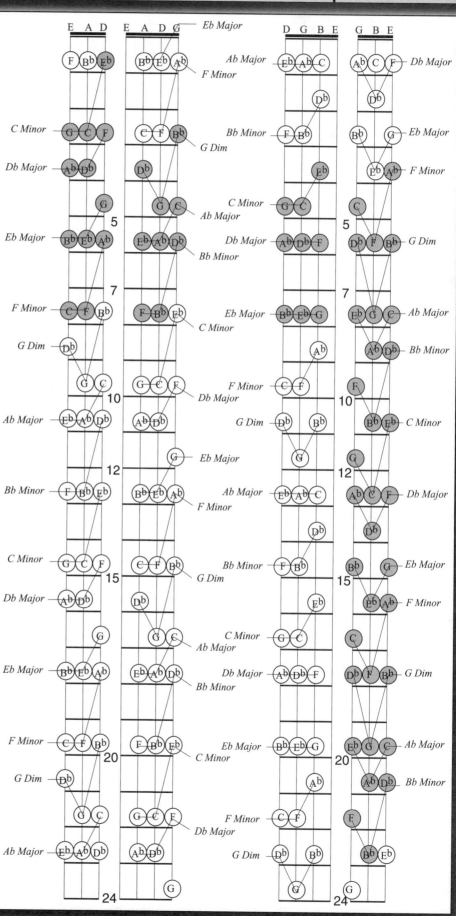

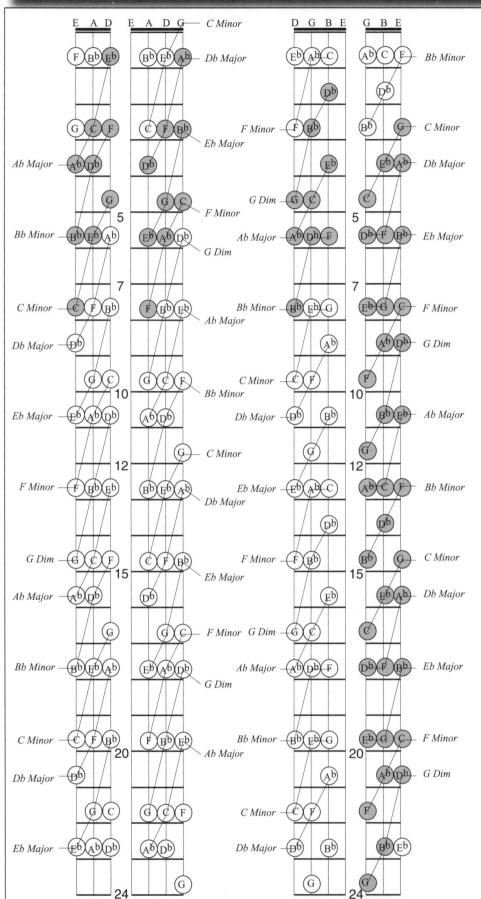

Root Position Triads

The root position triads are constructed by stacking the first, third and fifth degrees of the scale in that order. The root position is easy to relate to the scale because the triad is based on the tonic note. Notice that the gray triads are based on the notes of the scale for the first four strings. I have said this before and I continue to say it, because it is easy to forget. There is considerable power in combining the triads with the scale.

Since the root note dictates the name of the chord and these triads are based on the root note, the relationship between triads and scales is easier to understand.

Have you noticed that if you play the same chord one string over, very often you are three or four degrees up the scale. Also the fingerings are the same in many instances. Most of the time when you apply this information, you will not play the chords as a scale. You will mix them up and select specific chords based on the sound you are trying to create.

Many times the chords four or five degrees higher relate well. An example is the relationship between the tonic chord and the fifth or dominant chord. It is typical to migrate from the tonic chord right to the fifth chord. A typical rock rhythm is the one, five, four progression. In other words you play the tonic chord, then the five chord and then the four chord.

By thinking about the neighboring triads, this kind of movement can be identified and applied to create many different progressions using a standard progression such as the one, five, four.

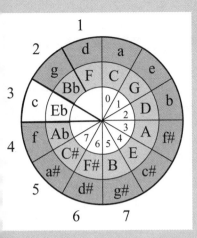

The Keys Of E♭ Major And C Minor

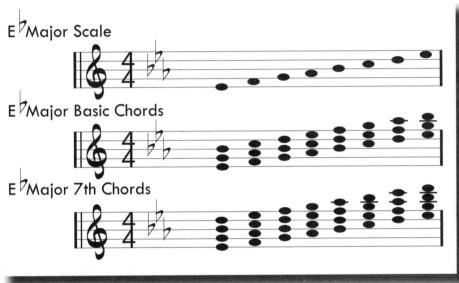

E♭ Major Scale

E♭ Major Basic Chords

E♭ Major 7th Chords

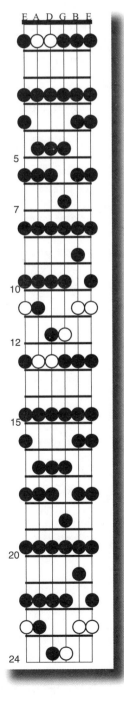

I	II	III	IV	V	VI	VII
Tonic	**Super Tonic**	**Mediant**	**Subdominant**	**Dominant**	**Submediant**	**Leading Tone**
Eb Major	F Minor	G Minor	Ab Major	Bb Major	C Minor	D Dim

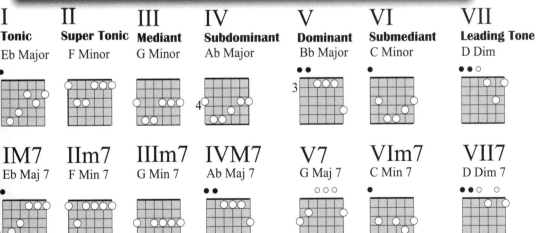

IM7	IIm7	IIIm7	IVM7	V7	VIm7	VII7
Eb Maj 7	F Min 7	G Min 7	Ab Maj 7	G Maj 7	C Min 7	D Dim 7

Seventh Chords

The first row of chords are composed of the first, third and fifth degrees of the scale starting on the chord root note. The second row builds on the first row by adding a seventh degree to some of the chords and notice the difference. The addition of the seventh degree will turn the chord into a seventh chord and add a very distinct flavor. The seventh chords are made up of the one, third, fifth and seventh degrees.

Practice

If you want to know the true secret of how a guitarist becomes excellent, the answer is actually very simple. **Practice!** Actually it would be more accurate to say quality time spent playing and exploring the guitar. Creating the necessary time and deciding what to do with it are the strategic concerns behind developing and building solid skills.

One of the main reasons scales are so helpful is that scales will increase your hand strength and accuracy far beyond what you might think they will. In fact I don't think you ever stop increasing your skill level over the course of a lifetime. After playing scales for 25 years, I still see things I continue to do better and I still refine certain skills.

After a few years, playing the guitar actually becomes a physiological study more than anything else. Look at it this way, the guitar never changes, the person does. This is actually a study in changing the response from your body and mind. Your main tool in refining your bodily response is practice and how you spend your time on the guitar.

What Happens When You Practice

The quality of your exercises and practice sessions will directly affect how much you accomplish and what effect it will have on your body and mind. When you practice a few things happen as a part of the process.

1. You develop your muscle groups. Your hands and fingers start to build up muscle mass. Your muscle groups begin to grow so accustomed to cradling and playing a guitar that a level of comfort becomes established.

2. You develop more specific coordination. Once you play a scale or chord progression 40 or 50 times you start to develop a sense of coordination. Your fingers start to anticipate what they are going to do next and then they start to increase the efficiency of the moves. The muscle memory you are developing will help get the process started and headed in the right direction.

3. Your hands and fingers start working together as a team. Individual coordination sets up the beginning of all your fingers working together as well as an increase in your ability to hold your hand in the exact, correct position, which will provide even greater efficiency to your fingers. This cycle of steady improvements happens quietly. No one sees it, it is a hidden effect that continually works to allow you to gain higher levels of control.

4. You train your mind to understand what is important. When this happens, you are well on your way. When your mind begins to be able to tell your fingers what to do and your fingers respond in a way that produces close to the desired results, you will start the process of obtaining absolute control over what is happening. At this point mistakes and miscues start to disappear. The rhythm of a song tightens up and a crispness and higher level of control occurs.

5. You then develop and start to refine a specific response to playing the instrument. After the mechanics are in place, you still increase your level of control. Eventually you obtain enough control that you can just pick up the instrument and play at a high level right away. Your style is in place and your level of confidence is growing.

6. You develop a sense of timing and you begin to associate what you are playing with what you are hearing. This effect is a combination of playing and practicing and growing your understanding. If you work out in C major heavily and you employ lots of finger picking and chording as well as scale work, you will recognize the key when you hear songs that employ it. You will recognize the tonal characteristics of the notes as you hear them. This ability can easily help you to know what position of the fretboard the artist is working from. You can even distinguish a B note played on the G string from one played on the D string. This can help you determine the nuances of songs as they pull out certain quirks in the music. These are very high level skills that will only show up after intense practice over many months.

The level of exactness that a fine guitarist develops will go far beyond what an average person experiences. Your body is set up to deliver this high level of control, but you must put in the time and high quality practice to develop this response.

Practicing And Playing With These Chords

You want to allow your fingers to get to know these chords by playing them! Sometimes you are not correcting anything wrong, you are just visiting the configurations and playing them. Repeating progressions and leads is something that everyone must do thousands of times. A very big part of playing guitar is repeating things and refining them. One of the reasons I suggest playing songs after scales and chording exercise is to limber up your fingers and tighten the exact timing of each note. Playing songs after your fingers have practiced will help you to concentrate on eliminating mistakes and executing correctly. Your response will be much better. All guitarists start out not knowing how to play. Practice makes all of them better. Play these and all the other chords as many times as you can. There is no upper limit. Make up new exercises often.

Right Hand Exercises

Pick any cascade below and play the chords from lowest to highest. Then when you can easily play them, do it and instead of strumming each chord, pick each note. Here are some exercises. Use either flat picking or finger picking or both.

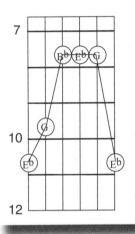

1. Play any four strings up the chord (from lowest to highest) and repeat this for 20 minutes.

Example: Eb, G, Bb, Eb on lowest four strings.

2. Play an arpeggio up and down and then repeat.

Example: Eb, G, Bb, Eb, Bb, G, Eb on lowest four strings.
Example: Bb, Eb, G, Eb, G, Eb, Bb. on highest four strings.

Pick any pattern of picking you may currently use and apply it to these cascades. If it is too hard to use these cascades, try the triads in the next section. Three string chords make it easier to concentrate on the right hand.

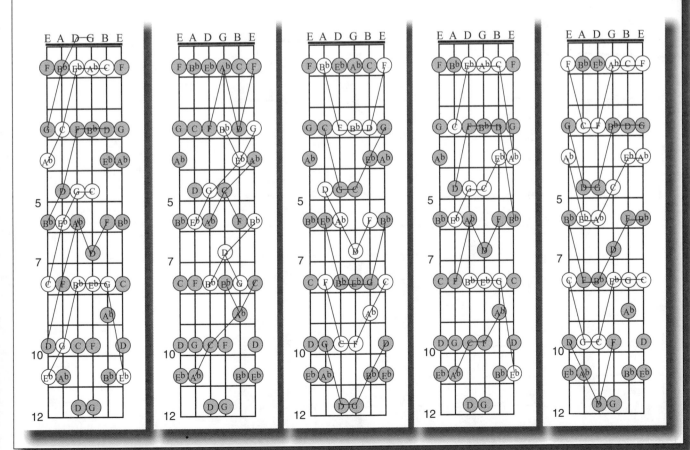

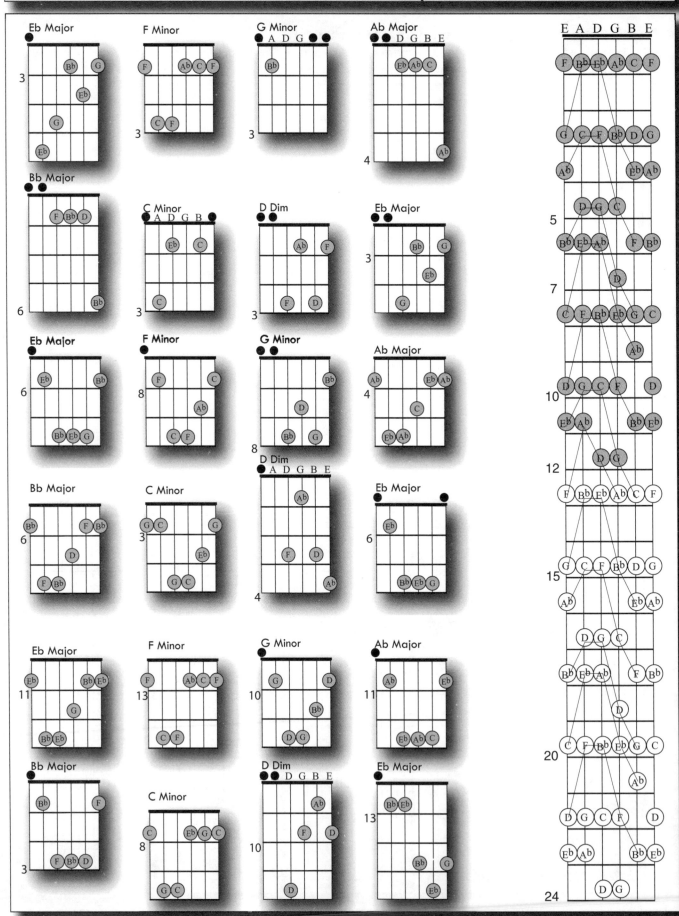

Seventh Chords

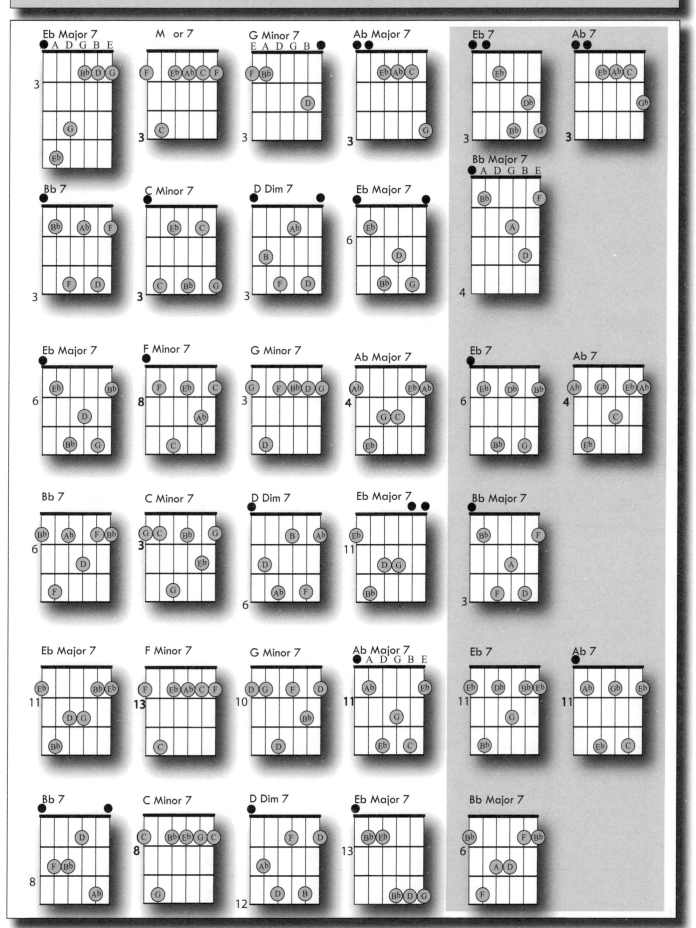

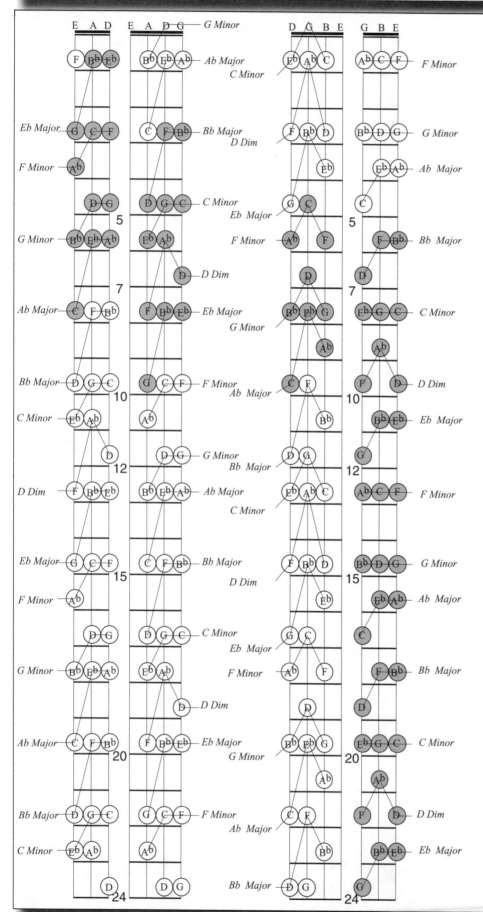

First Inversion Triads

The lowest three strings start with the tonic chord. I like this because it is a logical place to start and end the progression of chords.

Notice that the progression of chords is maj, min, min, maj, maj, min, dim. Also notice how the forms are consistent for the different types of chords. The minor chords all use the typical minor form. The major chords use the same form as tonic. This is a good example of the logical ordering of chords and the natural progression of the scale.

An interesting thing to note is that within the first five frets, all the chords are present except C Minor. If you want to look at the second inversion, you will see that the C minor is present below the fifth fret there.

This is valuable because you never have to go far to play any chord.

C Minor
The Relative Minor

Many people mix up the major and minor keys that share the same name. Many times I have been speaking about the key of C major and someone thought I meant the key of C minor.

They are totally different keys and mixing them up can have disastrous consequences. If you try to mix a progression in C major and a lead in C minor, you probably will not like the mix.

Some people will solo in the key of A minor over progressions in several different keys. Although this approach may yield some benefits, it is strictly hit or miss. Improvising without knowing exactly what key the rest of the musicians are in, will lead to mistakes.

Second Inversion Triads

The second inversion triads lead with the fifth degree. The progression is five, one, three. The second inversion has a particularly good use when extending the triad to include the seventh degree.

Advanced Study

This is a diagram of the lowest four strings using the rules of the second inversion. Now the seventh degree of the scale has been added. The triads are now composed of the first, third, fifth and seventh degree of the chord.

Notice the seventh degree is within easy reach when playing the other notes of the chords. The second inversion uses a combination of notes that facilitates the addition of this degree.

These are major and minor seventh chords. These chords maintain the same intervals and now place a new third on top of the one, three and five notes.

Seventh Chords

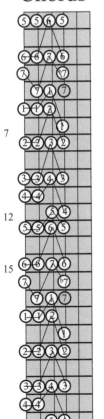

However there is a problem with the diminished seventh chord. In order to maintain three diminished triads, the seventh degree must be flatted. If you add a major third on top of the diminished triad, you would have a half diminished seventh chord. It is at this point that the subject enters into advanced study. It is also the first time we have altered the pattern to accommodate a chord!

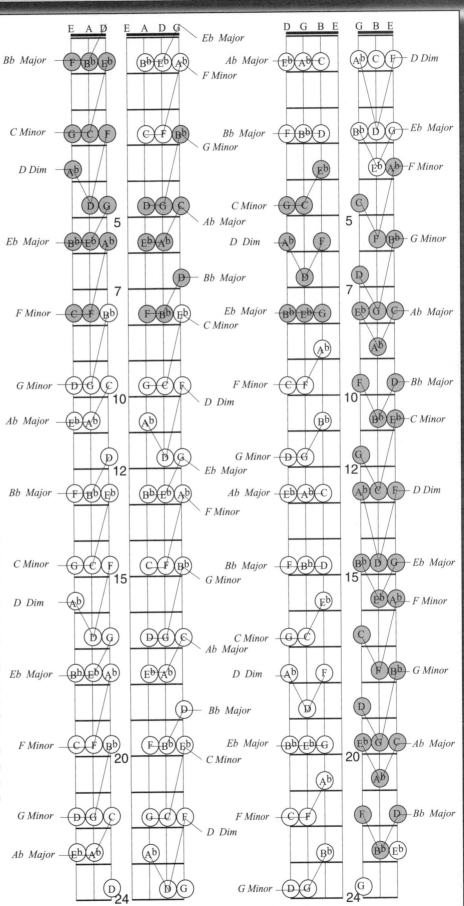

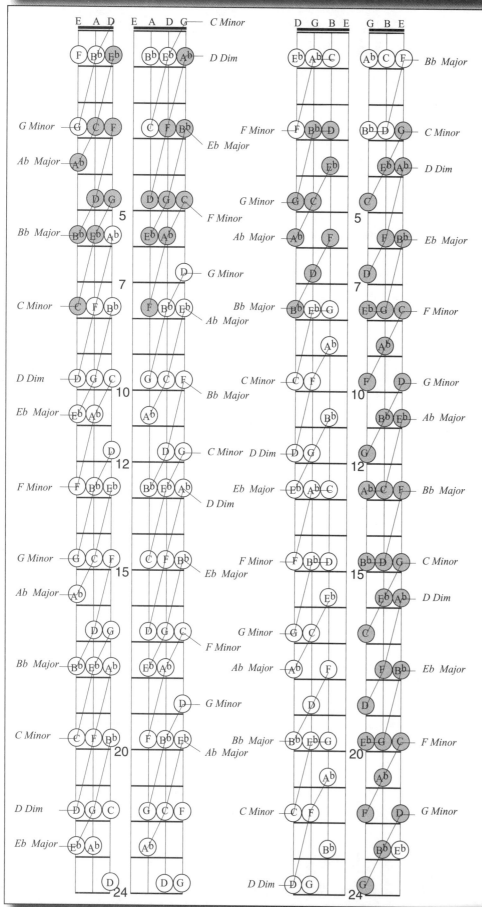

Advanced Study

We have seen the rules of music violate the diatonic pattern. The diminished seventh chord did violate the pattern so that three consecutive diminished triads could be formed. Because of the whole steps and half steps necessary to form a diatonic key, the occurrence of three consecutive diminished triads will not happen without violating the pattern.

The example of seventh chords on the previous page uses major and minor seventh chords because they do not violate the pattern. However seventh chords come in many different flavors, some by their very nature will violate the pattern!

This violation will use notes outside of the diatonic pattern. At this point we must consider all the notes, not just the notes of the pattern. We have come a great distance by observing the standard spacing of notes in a diatonic key. It is that base of information that will serve you well if you expand your study to include the more elaborate chord configurations.

We have said that altering the pattern is okay, as long as you know how you are going to do it. The intent of this book is to use visual information to explain how and why music is expressed on a guitar. The information is centered around the basics of theory and the direct application for the guitar.

Uncle Tim's Teaching Center

If you are looking for new material that will build on this series of books, then check out Uncle Tim's Teaching Center. There you will find eBooks, lessons, flash animations, videos and additional chord libraries that will build on the base of knowledge presented here. Uncle Tim's Teaching Center is the next step in your learning process.

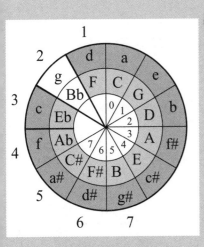

The Keys Of B♭ Major And G Minor

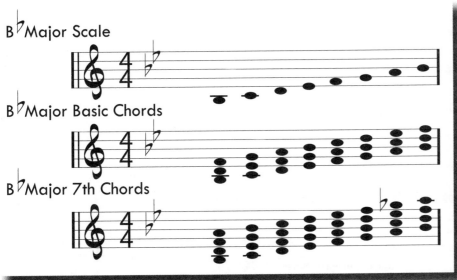

B♭ Major Scale

B♭ Major Basic Chords

B♭ Major 7th Chords

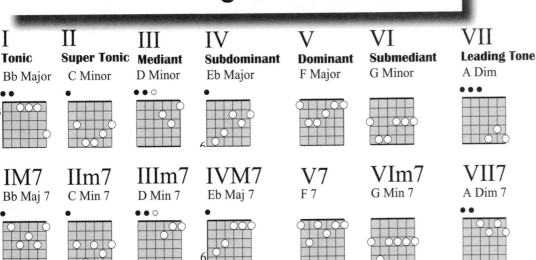

I	II	III	IV	V	VI	VII
Tonic	**Super Tonic**	**Mediant**	**Subdominant**	**Dominant**	**Submediant**	**Leading Tone**
Bb Major	C Minor	D Minor	Eb Major	F Major	G Minor	A Dim

IM7	IIm7	IIIm7	IVM7	V7	VIm7	VII7
Bb Maj 7	C Min 7	D Min 7	Eb Maj 7	F 7	G Min 7	A Dim 7

The Relative Minor

The sixth degree chord is the relative minor. This chord relates very heavily towards tonic. In fact, it uses the exact same scale and can be used as a bridge in songs to transition to another progression in the major key. You can also slip into the relative minor key and play a progression that relates to the relative minor. Returning to the related major key will be easy and sound logical.

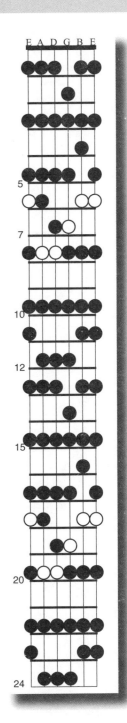

Expanding The Knowledge Base

Once the basic chords are understood, you can begin to insert additional elements and change the chords to include more notes and flavor.

Seventh chords can also be found cascading down fretboards just like basic triads. In fact, many different kinds of chords are available in this form. Triads can help to bridge chords with accents notes and chord fragments. These mini-chords can be injected only for accents or used to guide the main chordal phrases.

Seventh Triads

The triads below are made by combining the 1, 3 and 7 notes to form seventh triads. Seventh chords are four note chords composed of the 1, 3, 5 and 7 notes so technically these are not seventh chords. The fifth is left out because in most cases it is predictable and will occupy the perfect fifth position. So we leave it out. The third is included because it differentiates the 7th triads from the minor 7th triads. The seventh note is of course added to create the additional flavor. The tonic is included to keep the sound of the triad anchored and more easily identified. With some creative time, I am sure you create very sophisticated rhythms.

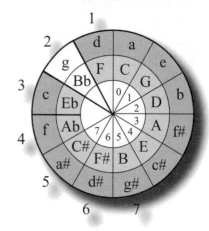

Another interesting exercise is to try creating different types of chords, like Sixth (1,3, 5 and 6 degree) chords, Suspended fourth chords (1, 4, 5) and other types of chords that have their roots in diatonic keys and are helpful in construction.

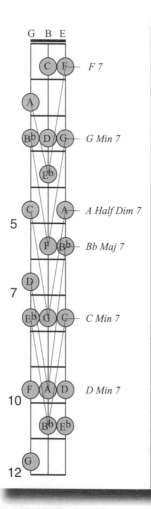

Thinking In Terms Of Degrees

The diagram on the left illustrates the notes shown as degrees for the key of Bb.

This can be helpful when you are trying to highlight the relationships between degrees. If you wanted to create some Bb major chords just start connecting the 1, 3 and 5 degrees. A Bb major chord will have at least one note of each of the 1, 3 and 5 notes. You can have additional instances of these degrees but you cannot add any other degrees.

When you construct chords by connecting the dots between degrees, you have to remember what degrees are associated with what notes.

Bb	1
C	2
D	3
Eb	4
F	5
G	6
A	7

To connect a C minor 7th triad, just look for a C, Eb, Bb or a 2, 4, 1. Using degrees is like creating a code and deciphering it.

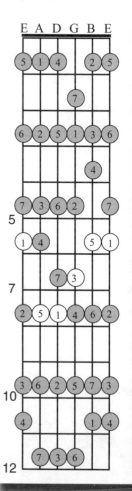

Evolving Basic Chords Into More Complex Forms

Once the basic chords are understood, changing them into more complex forms such as seventh chords is a great deal of fun. Seventh chords can be substituted for the base chord from which it was created at will. They are capable of adding a jazzy or sexy sound to the music just with their presence.

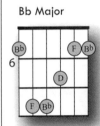
Bb Major

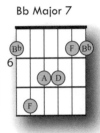
Bb Major 7

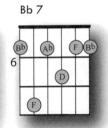
Bb 7

The chords to the left are the standard basic chords constructed for each key. The chord forms are used in every key. The cascades they come from are also present in every key, so once you know it, you can repeat it in the other keys with just a little work. The other chords on this page are seventh chords that are derived from the basic chords. There are three types of seventh chords here, the seventh or dominant chord, the major seventh and the minor seventh chord.

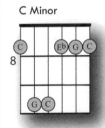
C Minor

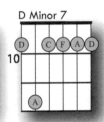
D Minor 7

Practice These Slowly

When played correctly, with all the notes ringing out, these chords sound wonderful. They add a fullness not found in the basic chords. And they also add secondary accent notes that elevate the sophistication of the sound.

When they are rushed and played poorly, they lose all of the elegance native to the chord. I suggest you start out slowly and bring out the fullness of each chord.

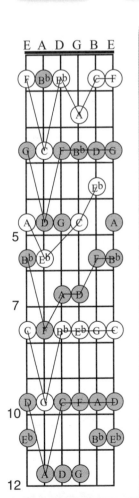

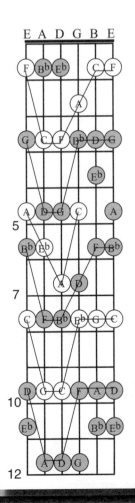

Practice playing the basic form and then morphing into the seventh form. Go back and forth. Play basic progressions and then substitute one or two seventh chords an see what it does to the sound. These chords will keep your music fresh and lively. They may seem harder to play at first, but that too will go away as your fingers realize how to play and hold them.

So the basic chords are the foundation of guitar. They can be used to create more complex chords and interchanged with these chords to create solid progressions. Everything starts with a well constructed musical progression and chords are the main tool for constructing this progression.

Seventh chords are built on top of the basic chords.

The Next Step May Be An eBook

By the time you read this, an advanced eBook will be available that will deal completely with these advanced chords and how they fit inside key structures.

The name is Uncle Tim, 7's, 9's, 11's and 13th's

It will be available along with many other eBooks
at http://www.uncletim.com
and http://www.eteachingcenter.com
You will also find errata sheets for this series.

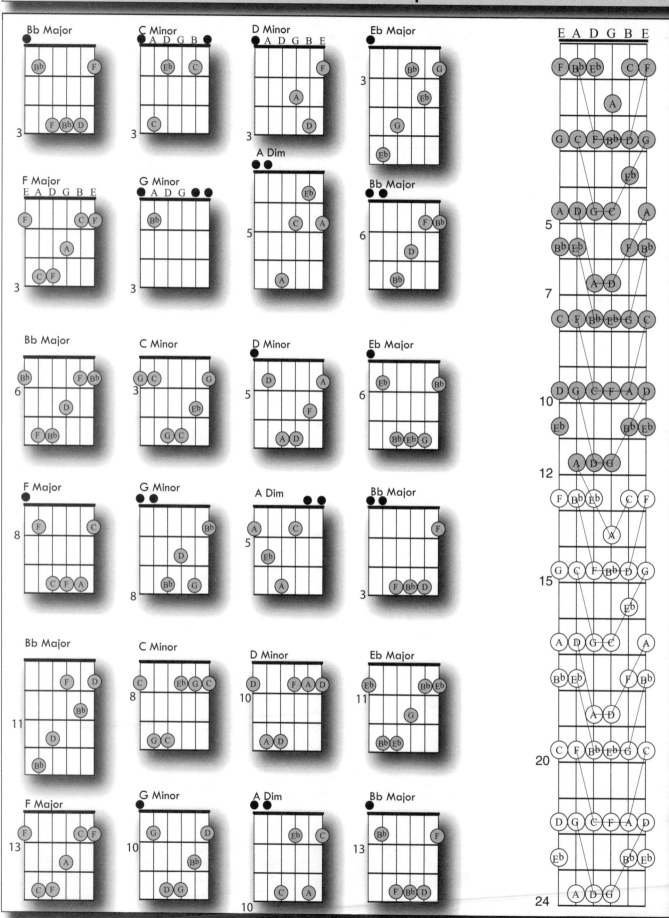

Seventh Chords

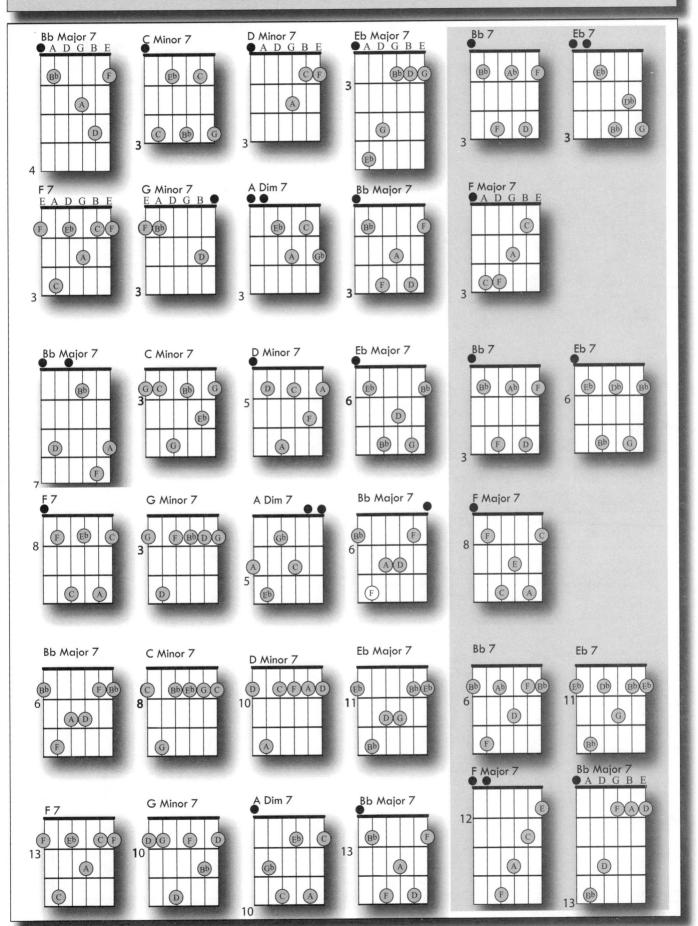

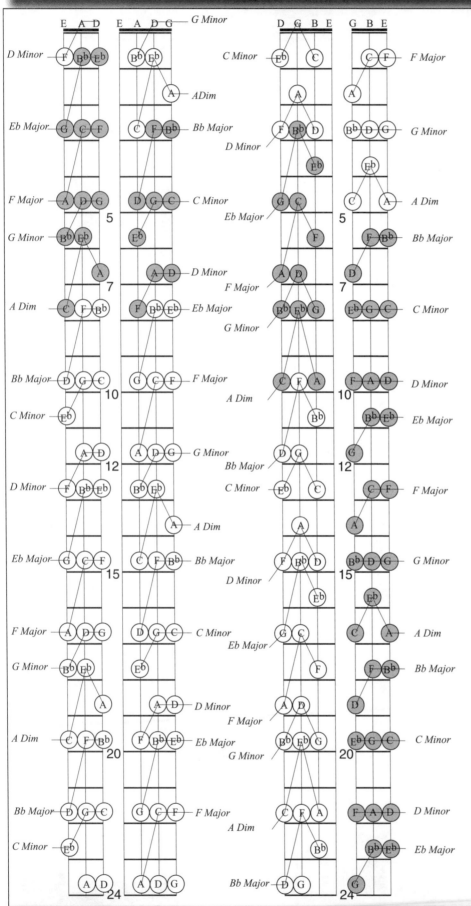

First Inversion Triads

To this point, we have discussed picking the notes with only simple picking patterns. If you have been able to pick the three notes and move up, down and across the fretboard, you may want to increase the picking difficulty.

Try playing arpeggios by starting with the lowest string, ascending to the highest string and then descending to the lowest note. One complete arpeggio would contain five strikes of the string. For the F major chord, the notes played would be A, C, F, C, A.

The trick is to play the notes smoothly. When you move to the next chord, you want to do so without a change to the rhythm developed in flat picking and without creating any additional sounds. As you practice this, you will build precision in your picking hand.

It may be easier to play the triads first and then pick the four, five and six string chords. When you add additional strings you complicate the process. It may be easier to use only three strings and concentrate more on the picking process.

First Inversion Triads

These triads are in the first inversion. The order of notes in the first inversion is 3, 5 and 1.

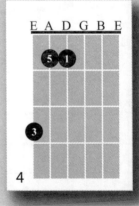

Second Inversion Triads

Have you noticed that the pattern is still working even though we have added sharps for each new key? Have you also noticed that since we started spelling these keys in terms of flats, we have been taking away a flat with each new key? The key of Bb has only two flats now, Bb and Eb. The next key is F and it will have only the Bb. Did you notice that we are still adding sharps to the seventh degree of each new key, but we can also describe it by subtracting a flat?

Advanced Study

The reason is that we are dealing with pure mathematics. By establishing the formula for a major scale as whole step, whole step, half step, whole step, whole step, whole step, half step intervals, we have mandated that the keys shall behave consistently and adhere to a mathematical formula for scale construction. Every key uses the same progression of whole steps and half steps. Each one just starts on different notes and adds sharps or flats to maintain the order of whole and half steps.

As the Circle of Fifths completes, we are left at the key of C again, and the whole process repeats itself. Remember after the next key, the key of F, is the key of C. Music is very repetitive.

2nd Inversion Triads

These triads are in the second inversion. The order of notes in the second inversion is 5, 1 and 3.

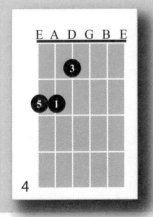

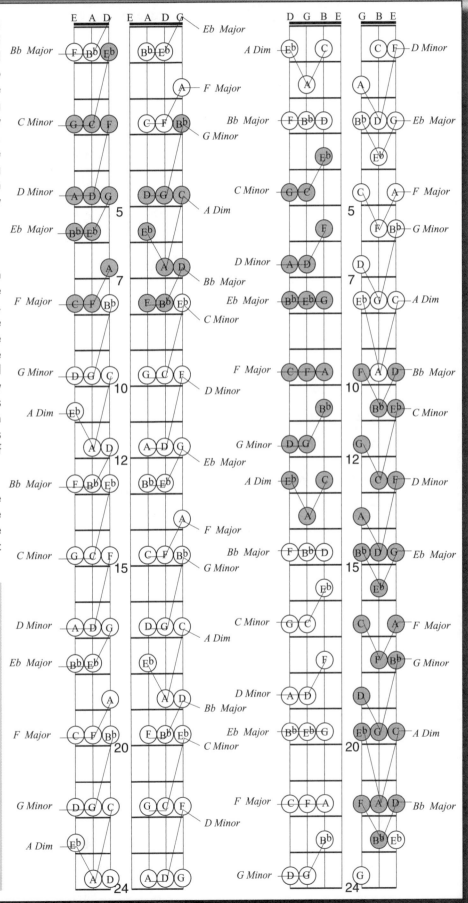

Root Inversion Triads For Bb Major

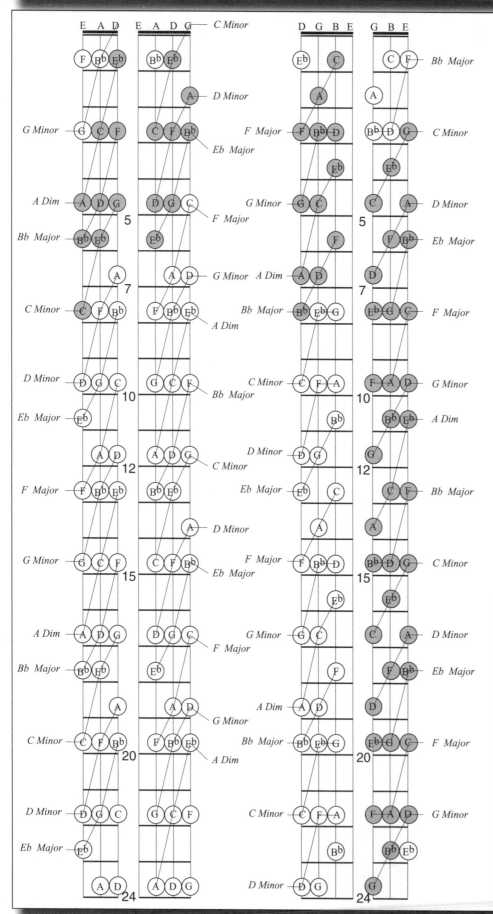

Root Position Triads

Finger picking can be a great right hand technique to work on with triads. When picking triads, I use the thumb for the lowest base note and the index and second fingers for the other two notes. It is good for exercising these two fingers and thumb, but the third (ring) finger does not get used at all. Playing four, five and six string chords will exercise the three fingers and thumb.

Try plucking all three strings at the same time and moving up and down the scale of chords. This can be an effective way of getting comfortable with the strings.

Root Inversion Triads

These triads are in the root position. The order of notes in the root inversion is 1, 3 and 5.

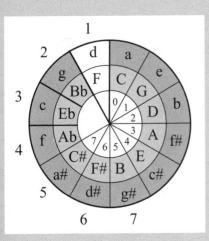

The Keys Of F Major And D Minor

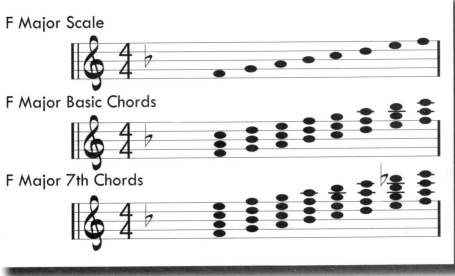

F Major Scale

F Major Basic Chords

F Major 7th Chords

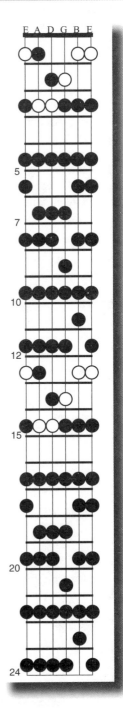

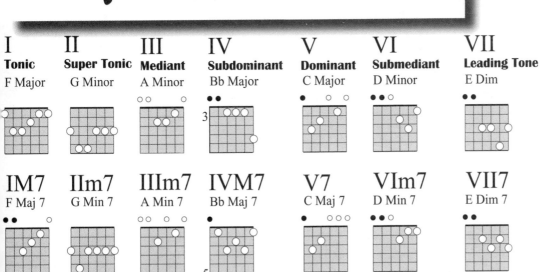

I	II	III	IV	V	VI	VII
Tonic	**Super Tonic**	**Mediant**	**Subdominant**	**Dominant**	**Submediant**	**Leading Tone**
F Major	G Minor	A Minor	Bb Major	C Major	D Minor	E Dim

IM7	IIm7	IIIm7	IVM7	V7	VIm7	VII7
F Maj 7	G Min 7	A Min 7	Bb Maj 7	C Maj 7	D Min 7	E Dim 7

The Circle Of Fifths

Notice the fifth degree of the Key of F is C. That of course is the next stop on the circle of fifths, and the progression will repeat itself. If you are playing through the circle of fifths, you will transfer to the next key by means of playing the dominant chord of the present key. From then on, you will be in a different key. You can play any progression you choose, but if you transfer to the next stop on the circle of fifths, you will do so by means of the dominant chord in the present key.

F Major

With this key you have completed one revolution of the circle of fifths. While looking at the details of each key and the overall integration of keys you can start to see how tightly the twelve keys are intertwined.

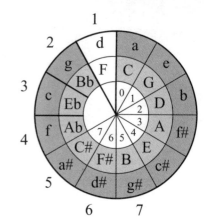

It still amazed me that this system has been around for centuries. This system of diatonic keys is well designed and has been exploited to create a library of songs that is too big to describe. Almost every song heard on the radio has it's roots in one of the twelve keys.

Working Within The Keys

Since everything in western keys is here, it makes sense to be able to use this information with your study of music and song creation. The diagram on the next page actually shows the notes of each key. Every note has been used as we cycled through the twelve major keys.

I suggest making sure you have a working knowledge of all the chords in each of these keys and of course I suggest you play the scales of each of these keys. The long term benefit is what you are after. You want to develop a strong tactile response and a working knowledge that allows for quick exploitation. This will be a time consuming commitment.

By now you have experienced many opportunities to understand and increase your understanding of the complete realm of diatonic keys. Let this happen over time. You will be using diatonic keys for some time if you continue to play music. If you take your time and grow your understanding over time you will gain the benefit of long term memory. Your knowledge will take on new meaning as the depth and complexity becomes working knowledge.

How To Practice Using This book

Technique exercises should be a part of every guitarist's workload. Technique exercises can be revisited whenever you feel the need to sharpen things up a bit. I regularly use this book for that. Here is how I usually use it.

One Inversion at a time. Try to visit every key using the same inversion. I start with the C major key and pick out one inversion. I go over it 40 or 50 times. I usually finger of flat pick scales of chords and work on getting the mechanics just right. Once I am satisfied with the results, I move to the next key.

One area of the fretboard at a time. Using this idea, I usually stay in one key and work out the different possibilities for one specific area of the guitar. Often it is the higher four strings towards the first five to seven frets. I usually start by working inside one inversion only and trying to get comfortable with the chords. Then I will work in another inversion and try to mix some chords and create some interesting combinations. Usually this is done with the first and second inversions. Then finally I will work in some root inversion triads and try to take advantage of the unique finger positions of the root inversion.

Using all three is a good idea if you want to explore an area in detail. It is always a good idea to move to another key and try it out there.

Scales with chords. I start by playing scales and after I am comfortable, I will add some chords to the end of the run. Always in the key and usually four or five. You can easily expand this to include an entire progression.

Chord Hunting. I use this when I am writing a song and looking to expand the passage by climbing or falling and working down a chordal line. If you are looking in a certain part of the fretboard for a chord, the inversions will probably give you some options. You should be able to find just about any chord in any part of the fretboard.

This is just a sampling of the ways I will practice using this material.

Once Around The Circle

At this point we have visited every key. If you take a look at the top of this illustration you will see it starts with the key of F major. We added that to the diagram when we were examining C major. We did this so you would see the circular nature of the circle of fifths. Now we are actually at F major and the very next key is C major.

The gray bars are positioned over the major chords. The idea is if you have this page open when you are cycling through the circle of fifths, you may be able to figure out what to play while you are playing.

So once we finish with this key, we will find ourselves back at C major and the circle will repeat.

We have worked through each key by moving to the fifth and then starting a new key based on the fifth of the existing key.

So this is how the circle of fifths works. It is the guide to diatonic keys.

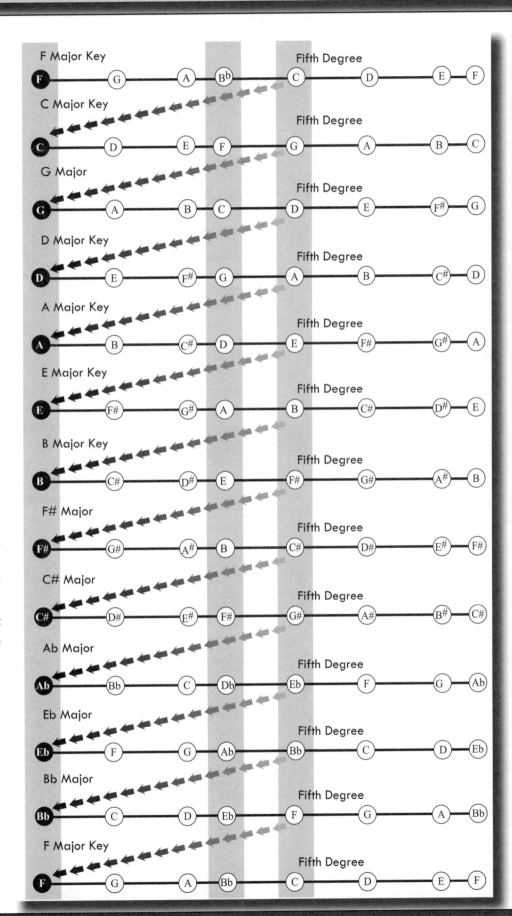

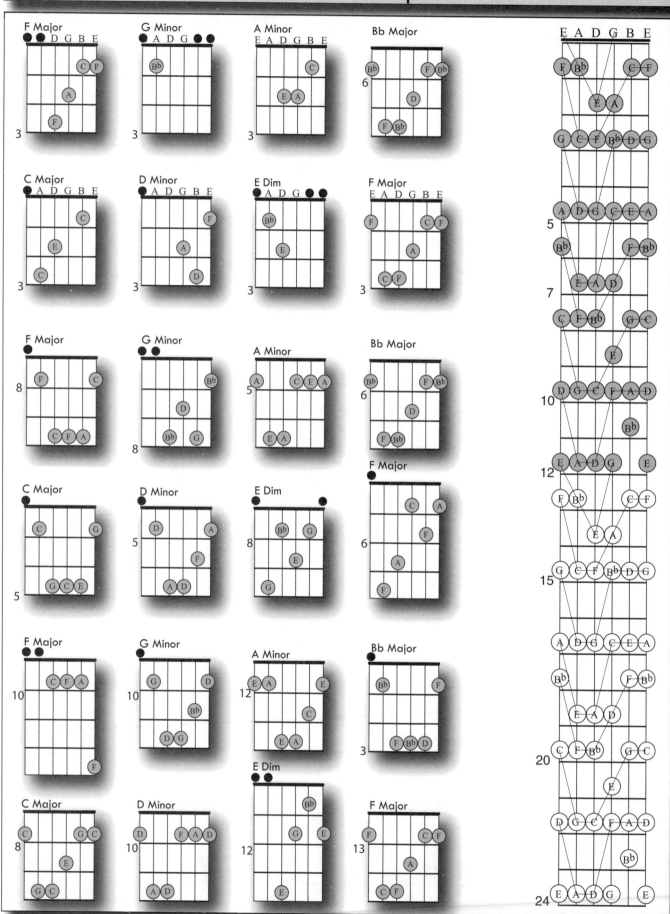

Seventh Chords

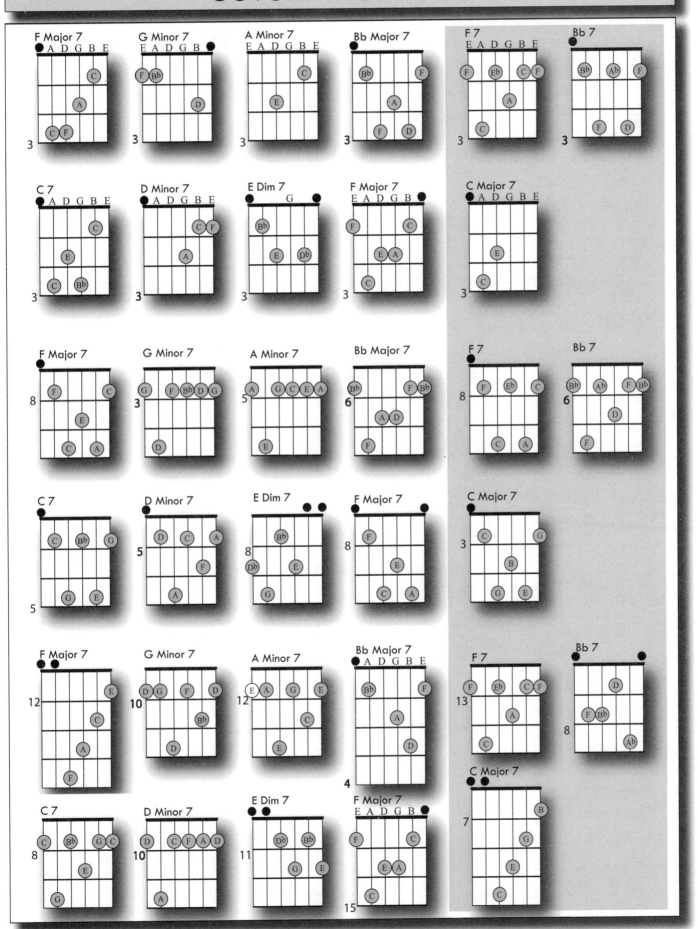

1st Inversion Triads For F Major

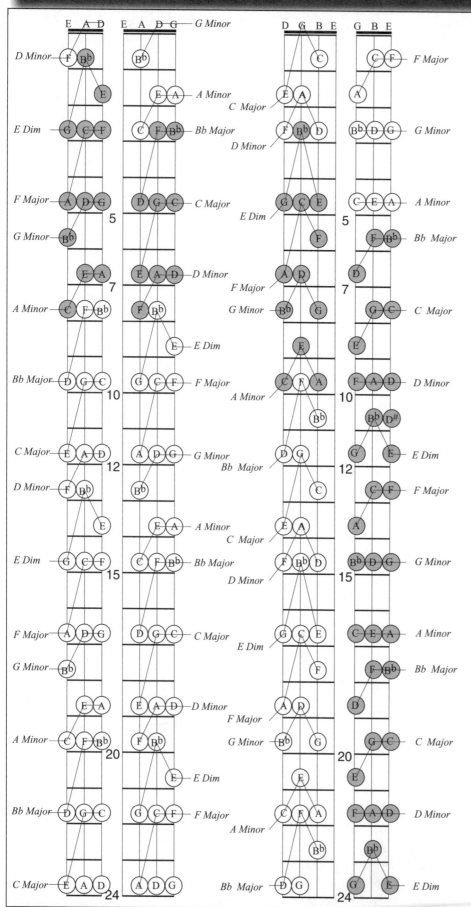

First Inversion Triads

Where are you with recall ability? Does the progression of chords come easily now? Are your fingers used to the next sequence of movement? Can you change keys and still recall the relationships between chords? Is the notion of tonality an integral part of your use of these chords?

As usual, these questions ask you to access how well you know this information and how well you can use it.

If you are an improvisational player, has it crept into your style or influenced your movement over the fretboard?

If you are a songwriter, has it given you new ideas for progressions and changes or secondary parts? Can you select chords that sound better than others based on the appropriate inversion for your needs?

If you are using this for general finger dexterity or an understanding of the instrument, can you play the chords cleanly and with no apparent prejudice towards certain fingers with certain chords? Are your favorite songs easier to play because of practice? Do you understand the fretboard and the layout of notes and chords? Can you combine scales and chords to form interesting passages? Has your personal style been changed because you are practicing new ideas?

Every person is influenced by what they play! If you play something long and hard enough, it will find a way to creep into your personal style. Welcome the change, but make sure you control the direction. If you are an improviser, you may be thinking that you do not want to control the direction, but in fact you do. If you are not getting the sound you like, you must provide enough control to change the subtle nature of your approach. We always try to supply control. The question is to what degree?

Second Inversion Triads

When you play the chords do you think about the first 34 pages? Those pages provide the information to build these chords. The laws of construction determine the repetitive nature of these chords. When you look at the progressions, do you notice the consistency of the major and minor chords? Do you try to spot the diminished chord?

Do you travel the same path up and down the neck? Do you have favorite areas in which to work? Have you combined short linear passages with some chords to produce a mixture of responses? Have you developed favorite combinations of these chords and played them in different keys? These are questions to make you think about how you use the information. Not all questions should be answered yes. But it is common for people to have the information and not get what they want! Why? Sometimes, it is a matter of taking time to combine your mental picture with the mechanics. Other times, it is a question of how you think about the information.

I have seen people who practice scales, but are unaware that they have a good foundation for improvisation! By thinking about things in new ways, we are able to apply information and break new ground. Sometimes, it can take a teacher to help. Other times, it is just necessary to play with someone who makes use of the information in a way that appeals to you.

Whatever the case, if you are trying to get to another level and you are having trouble seeing the path to achieve it, take time to examine what it is that you need to change. You might go to an instructor, taking definite goals you wish to achieve. Set up a plan that will yield the goal in question. Maybe it is just a small change in your technique that someone more advanced can point out. If you can take their advice and make a change, you may have found the missing link. When it happens, it feels great!

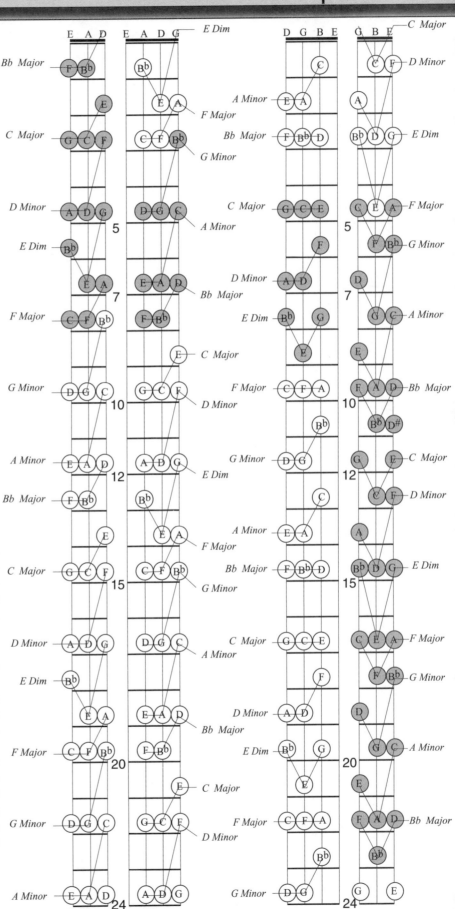

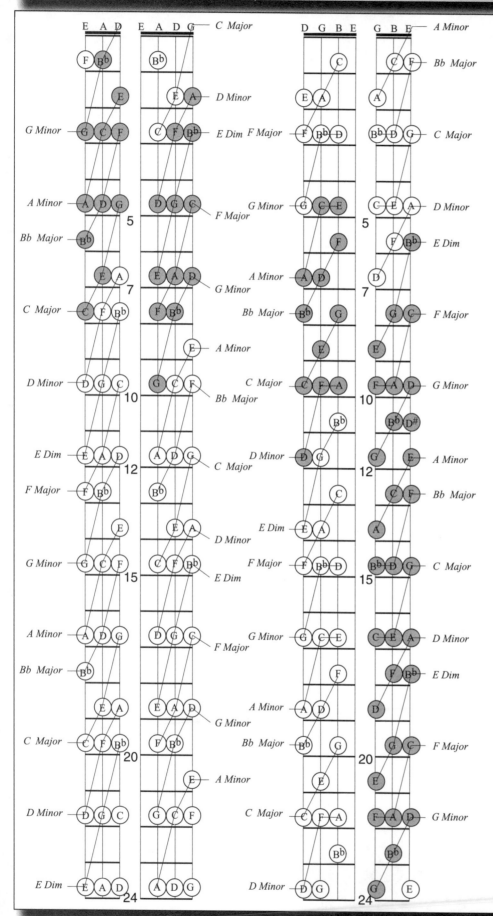

Root Position Triads

The root-position triads were the guiding force for me when I developed these maps! These chords were easy for me to understand, because they are built by means of the 1, 3 and 5 in that order. They were my first example of the natural order of the fretboard. For my personal uses, I favor the first inversion chords because of the sound and the feel of the chords. That is usually the inversion I work out of when I am exploring new ideas. If I were to use the other inversions more, my music would change.

Remember to reread the first 34 pages once in a while! The information will continually refresh your understanding of construction. As you go through time this information will become more familiar. Your fingers will continue to have an easier time, and you will continue to see the information in new ways.

If you have experienced some explosive growth, remember there is always more. The key is to practice information that can provide the foundation for the growth you are after. Finishing this book is not the end of your technical study. There is always something new that will interest you. The information that you attain will always spawn new questions. There are exciting, advanced ebooks that fit on top of this information, keep in touch!

Thank you for allowing me to participate in your music.

MOUNTAIN STUDIOS
Boulder CO
http://www.uncletim.com
E-mail uncletim@uncletim.com

Extend your study at
Uncle Tim's Teaching Center
http://www.eteachingcenter.com